GCSE English

The Merchant of Venice

by William Shakespeare

The Merchant of Venice offers life-and-death drama by the pound, but it can be a real challenge to flesh out your essays about it.

Not to worry. This brilliant Text Guide explains the whole thing — characters, language, structure, themes… the lot. And because it's a CGP book, we get straight to the point, with no needless rambling.

We've also included plenty of practice questions to test you on what you've learned, plus a section of advice on how to plan and write brilliant essays. So that's a weight off your shoulders, as Shylock might say.

The Text Guide

CONTENTS

CONTENTS

Section Four — Context and Themes

Section Five — Shakespeare's Techniques

Section Six — Exam Advice

The Characters in 'The Merchant of Venice'
'The Merchant of Venice' Cartoon

Published by CGP

Editors:
Alex Fairer
Louise McEvoy
Jack Tooth

Contributor:
Jude Vale

With thanks to Matt Topping and Paula Barnett for the proofreading.
With thanks to Ana Pungartnik for the copyright research.

Acknowledgements:

With thanks to Michal Daniel for permission to use the front cover image and the image on page 4.

With thanks to Alamy for permission to use the images on pages 1, 2, 5, 10, 20, 21, 38, 43 & 53.

With thanks to ArenaPAL for permission to use the images on pages 3, 17, 22, 26, 50 & 52.

With thanks to iStock.com for permission to use the image on page 1.

With thanks to Photostage for permission to use the images on pages 3, 4, 5, 7, 8, 11, 12, 14, 15, 16, 19, 27, 28, 31, 32, 33, 36, 37, 40, 46, 47, 49, 51 & 54.

With thanks to Rex Features for permission to use the images on pages 3, 6, 9, 18, 25, 29, 30, 41, 42 & 48.

With thanks to Shakespeare's Globe for permission to use the images on pages 3, 5, 13 & 39.

Image on page 3: Phoebe Pryce as Jessica and Ben Lamb as Lorenzo in The Merchant of Venice, directed by Jonathan Munby, at Shakespeare's Globe (2015). Photographer credit Manuel Harlan.

Image on page 5: Jonathan Pryce as Shylock and Dominic Mafham as Antonio in The Merchant of Venice, directed by Jonathan Munby, at Shakespeare's Globe (2015). Photographer credit Manuel Harlan.

Image on page 13: Phoebe Pryce as Jessica in The Merchant of Venice, directed by Jonathan Munby, at Shakespeare's Globe (2015). Photographer credit Manuel Harlan.

Image on page 39: Daniel Lapaine as Bassanio and Dominic Mafham as Antonio in The Merchant of Venice, directed by Jonathan Munby, at Shakespeare's Globe (2015). Photographer credit Manuel Harlan.

ISBN: 978 1 78294 849 0
Printed by Elanders Ltd, Newcastle upon Tyne.
Images and Clipart throughout the book from Corel® and Clipart.com.

Based on the classic CGP style created by Richard Parsons.

'The Merchant of Venice' and Shakespeare

'The Merchant of Venice' is about a merchant in debt

- *The Merchant of Venice* is a <u>comedy</u> about a <u>wealthy merchant</u> who borrows money from a <u>vengeful</u> Jewish <u>moneylender</u>. When he <u>fails to repay</u> the loan in time, he has to give up a <u>pound of his flesh</u>.

- After a dramatic court scene, the merchant is <u>saved</u>. The Jewish moneylender, however, is <u>ruined</u>.

- *The Merchant of Venice* is one of Shakespeare's most <u>controversial</u> plays. The <u>prejudice</u> shown towards the play's Jewish characters was <u>normal</u> in the 16th century, but it is <u>shocking</u> today.

The Merchant of Venice is about revenge and love

1) The play examines whether <u>revenge</u> is ever <u>justified</u>, or if it's better to show others <u>mercy</u>. Shakespeare presents mercy as a <u>divine</u> quality, and suggests that seeking revenge leads to <u>problems</u>.

2) Shakespeare uses the play to explore different types of <u>love</u> — <u>romantic relationships</u>, <u>male friendships</u> and <u>family love</u>. At times, these different types of love come into <u>conflict</u> with each other.

Granger Historical Picture Archive / Alamy Stock Photo

Shakespeare is the most famous writer in the English language

- William Shakespeare wrote at least <u>thirty-seven plays</u> and a lot of <u>poems</u>.

- He wrote some of the most <u>famous</u> plays in the English language, including <u>comedies</u> (such as *Twelfth Night*), <u>tragedies</u> (such as *Romeo and Juliet* and *Hamlet*) and <u>histories</u> (such as *Richard III*).

- In spite of its <u>dark</u> subject matter, *The Merchant of Venice* is classed as a <u>comedy</u> (see p.46).

- The play was written in the <u>1590s</u>, but it was inspired by a range of <u>written sources</u>, as well as <u>real-life</u> events. Some of these were from the <u>16th century</u>, but some were from <u>long before</u> then. For example, the idea of the <u>test of the caskets</u> came from a collection of <u>stories</u> written in the <u>13th or 14th century</u>.

1564	Born in <u>Stratford-upon-Avon</u>, Warwickshire.
1582	Married <u>Anne Hathaway</u>.
1583-85	Had three children — Susanna, Hamnet and Judith.
1585-92	Began an <u>acting career</u> in <u>London</u>.
1589-1613	Wrote most of his plays.
1600	First edition of '<u>The Merchant of Venice</u>' printed.
1616	Died, aged 52.

© iStockphoto.com/claudiodivizia

Background Information

'The Merchant of Venice' is set in Venice

Here's a map of the <u>main locations</u> in the play, showing where all the <u>important action</u> happens.

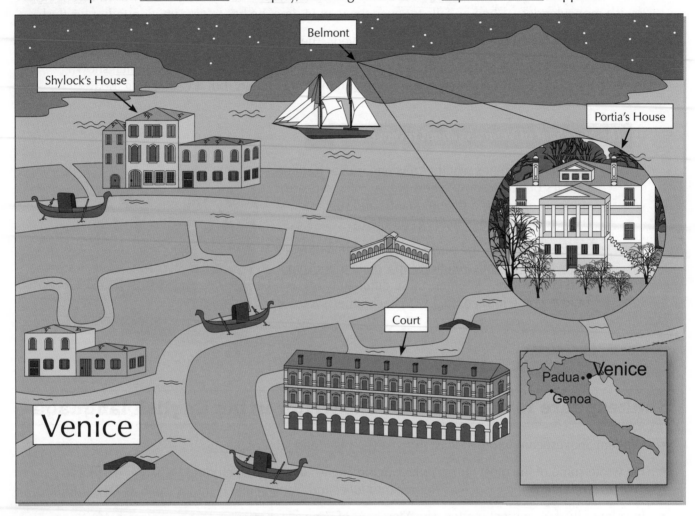

Theatre was an important form of entertainment

The rebuilt Globe Theatre in London.

© Peter Phipp/Travelshots.com / Alamy Stock Photo

- There was no <u>TV</u>, <u>radio</u> or <u>internet</u> in Shakespeare's time, so going to the <u>theatre</u> was really popular.

- The theatre wasn't just for <u>rich</u> people — Shakespeare's audiences included <u>servants</u> and <u>labourers</u>. Audiences could get quite <u>rowdy</u> during performances.

- The <u>poorer</u> people in the audience stood in <u>front</u> of the stage — if it rained, they got wet. The <u>richer</u> people sat in the <u>covered galleries</u> above.

- Shakespeare's theatre company, the <u>King's Men</u> (previously called the <u>Lord Chamberlain's Men</u>), performed in the <u>Globe Theatre</u> in London. This was <u>rebuilt</u> in 1997.

- It was <u>illegal</u> for <u>women</u> to act, so the women's parts were played by young <u>boys</u> (even Portia...).

Introduction

Who's Who in 'The Merchant of Venice'

Antonio...

... is a successful merchant. He borrows money to help Bassanio, but his life is at risk when he can't repay it.

Bassanio...

... is Antonio's close friend. He asks Antonio for money so that he can woo Portia — the woman he loves.

Portia...

... is a clever, rich heiress. She marries Bassanio and saves Antonio by disguising herself as a young lawyer.

Shylock...

... is a Jewish moneylender. He lends money to Antonio, then seeks revenge when Antonio fails to repay it.

Jessica...

... is Shylock's daughter. She marries Lorenzo and becomes a Christian to escape her Jewish origins.

Nerissa...

... is Portia's lady-in-waiting. She's close to Portia and helps her to save Antonio's life. She marries Gratiano.

Lorenzo...

... is a friend of Antonio and Bassanio who's in love with Jessica. He runs away with her so that they can marry.

Gratiano...

... is also friends with Antonio and Bassanio. He falls in love with Nerissa and marries her.

Plot Summary

Photo copyright © Michal Daniel

'The Merchant of Venice'… what happens when?

The Merchant of Venice needs to be as familiar to you as your favourite socks. This little recap of the <u>main events</u> will help you on your way, but it's no substitute for reading the play. There's no escaping that I'm afraid...

Act One — Bassanio prepares to woo Portia

- <u>Bassanio</u> wants to marry <u>Portia</u>. He doesn't have enough <u>money</u> to compete with her other suitors, so he asks <u>Antonio</u> if he can <u>borrow</u> some from him.

- Antonio <u>agrees</u> to help Bassanio, but he won't have the money until his <u>ships return</u>. He gives Bassanio permission to take out a <u>loan</u> in his name instead.

- Portia complains to <u>Nerissa</u> about having <u>no say</u> in who she <u>marries</u>. Her father has set up a test for her suitors involving <u>three caskets</u> (small chests) — she can only marry a man who chooses the <u>correct</u> one.

© Donald Cooper/photostage

- Bassanio and Antonio <u>negotiate</u> a loan with <u>Shylock</u>. Antonio is <u>prejudiced</u> against Shylock, and Shylock <u>hates</u> him. Shylock sees the loan as an opportunity for <u>revenge</u> — he demands a <u>pound of Antonio's flesh</u> if it isn't repaid <u>in time</u>.

- Antonio <u>accepts</u> Shylock's terms, <u>confident</u> that his ships will return to Venice <u>soon</u>.

Act Two — Jessica abandons Shylock

- Portia welcomes the <u>Prince of Morocco</u> to Belmont.

- <u>Lancelet</u> stops serving <u>Shylock</u> and is taken on by <u>Bassanio</u> instead. As he leaves Shylock's house, <u>Jessica</u> gives him a <u>letter</u> to take to Lorenzo.

- Lorenzo gets Jessica's <u>letter</u> and finds out she plans to <u>escape</u> that night. He gathers his friends to help him <u>take her away</u> while Shylock is out.

- Jessica's escape goes <u>smoothly</u>. Jessica <u>steals</u> a small fortune from Shylock before she leaves. She and Lorenzo go away to get <u>married</u>. Meanwhile, Bassanio and Gratiano <u>set sail</u> for Belmont.

© Donald Cooper/photostage

- The Prince of Morocco <u>attempts</u> and <u>fails</u> the test of the caskets.

- The audience finds out that Shylock is <u>devastated</u> by Jessica's <u>betrayal</u>.

- <u>Salerio</u> and <u>Solanio</u> discuss a <u>rumour</u> that one of Antonio's ships has <u>run aground</u> — it's got stuck in <u>shallow waters</u> and <u>can't return</u>. It seems <u>unlikely</u> that Antonio will be able to repay his loan <u>on time</u>.

- Another suitor takes the test of the caskets — the <u>Prince of Aragon</u>. Like the Prince of Morocco, he <u>fails</u>.

Act Three — Antonio's in trouble

- Tubal tells Shylock that Jessica is spending his money recklessly and has sold a precious ring. Shylock is angry and upset, but cheers up when he hears Antonio has lost another of his ships.

- Bassanio arrives at Belmont and passes the test of the caskets — he's now engaged to Portia. Gratiano and Nerissa also get engaged.

- Portia and Nerissa give Bassanio and Gratiano rings. The men swear to hold onto them forever.

- News reaches Belmont that Antonio couldn't repay his loan on time. Bassanio and Gratiano leave for Venice.

- Antonio is arrested. He appeals to Shylock for mercy, but Shylock ignores him. He resigns himself to his fate.

- Portia and Nerissa pretend they're going to stay at a monastery, but secretly follow their husbands to Venice.

Acts Four and Five — Portia comes to the rescue

- Antonio's trial begins. It's clear that Antonio has breached the terms of his loan, making it almost certain that Shylock will get his pound of flesh. Antonio's only hope is for Shylock to show mercy.

- Portia and Nerissa enter the courtroom disguised as a male lawyer and his assistant. Portia lectures Shylock on the importance of mercy, but this doesn't change Shylock's mind — he demands justice.

- Portia saves Antonio by pointing out that Shylock can't take Antonio's flesh without illegally taking blood. Shylock is punished for trying to kill Antonio — he has to give up lots of money and become a Christian.

- Still in disguise, Portia asks Bassanio for his ring as a reward for saving Antonio. He hesitates, but gives in. Nerissa persuades Gratiano to do the same.

- The main characters (apart from Shylock) gather at Belmont. Only Portia and Nerissa know the true identity of the 'lawyer' and his 'assistant'.

- Portia and Nerissa trick their husbands. They scold Bassanio and Gratiano for giving their rings away, before putting them out of their misery by revealing that they were the lawyer and assistant all along.

- The play ends on a joyful note. Antonio learns that his ships returned after all, and Lorenzo and Jessica are told they'll inherit everything from Shylock when he dies. All of the couples are happily reconciled.

In for a penny, in for a pound — of flesh...

Once you're confident that you know what happens in the play, you're ready to start Section One. If you're still not sure about the plot or want a break from revision, have a look at *The Merchant of Venice* cartoon at the back of the book.

How Plays Work

Lots of people will tell you that Shakespeare's the hardest thing you'll have to study for English, and they're probably right — but it should become a bit easier when you've read all the helpful points in this section.

'The Merchant of Venice' is meant to be watched — not read

1) *The Merchant of Venice* is a <u>play</u>. A play tells a story by <u>showing</u> it to you.

2) When you <u>read</u> the play, it's often pretty hard to <u>follow</u> what's going on. Try to <u>imagine</u> what's happening and how the people would <u>speak</u> and <u>act</u> — it should all start to make a lot more sense.

3) If you can, try to see the play <u>on stage</u>. If not, watch a <u>film</u> version to get an idea of the <u>story</u>.

4) But remember to <u>read the play</u> as well — films often <u>cut scenes</u> and <u>change</u> the language, so it's <u>dangerous</u> to rely on them too much.

'The Merchant of Venice' is a comedy

The Merchant of Venice is one of Shakespeare's <u>most famous</u> plays. In many ways, it's a <u>typical comedy</u>...

- It ends <u>happily</u> — Antonio is <u>saved</u> and all three couples are <u>reconciled</u>.
- There are plenty of <u>disguises</u> and <u>mistaken identities</u>.
- There are characters who are only there to <u>create humour</u>, like Lancelet.

...but it has some <u>tragic</u> bits too:

- The play addresses serious topics like <u>justice</u>, <u>mercy</u> and <u>revenge</u>.
- Antonio comes close to being <u>brutally murdered</u> on stage in Act 4, Scene 1.
- The play contains a lot of <u>hatred</u> and <u>abuse</u>, particularly towards Shylock.

© Jane Hobson/REX/Shutterstock

Pay attention to the stage directions

When you're reading the play, look at the <u>stage directions</u> — they're little phrases in *italics* that tell the actors <u>what</u> to do, <u>when</u> to come in and when to <u>leave</u> the stage.

These are the really <u>common</u> stage directions in <u>Shakespeare</u>:

Enter	=	when someone <u>comes onto</u> the stage
Exit	=	when one person <u>leaves</u> the stage
Exeunt	=	when <u>more</u> than one person <u>leaves</u>
Aside	=	when a character is <u>talking</u> to <u>themselves</u>, the <u>audience</u> or a <u>particular</u> character, but <u>not all</u> characters on stage can <u>hear</u>

EXAM TIP

Think of the play as more than just words on a page...

Shakespeare didn't expect people to sit at home reading his plays — he wrote them to be performed in a theatre. When you're writing about the play, it's important to think about how it would look on stage.

How to Understand Shakespeare's Language

Shakespeare's plays can be more confusing than a fox and ferret convention, especially all the strange ye olde language. But there are certain ways of reading it so it makes more sense — here's how it's done...

The play is written in poetry and prose

1) Some of the play is written in <u>poetry</u> — but the poetry doesn't always rhyme.

2) The poetry is the bits where all the lines are <u>roughly the same length</u>, and each line starts with a <u>capital letter</u>. It <u>looks like this</u>:

> "Beshrew me but I love her heartily;
> For she is wise, if I can judge of her,
> And fair she is, if that mine eyes be true,"
>
> Act 2, Scene 6

3) Some bits of the play are in <u>prose</u> — prose is normal sentences without any set rhythm.

4) Characters with a <u>low status</u>, like Lancelet and his father, <u>usually</u> speak in <u>prose</u>.

5) Sometimes, the <u>main characters</u> speak in <u>prose</u> too — Portia and Nerissa use prose in Act 1, Scene 2.

For more on poetry and prose, see Section 5.

Don't stop reading at the end of each line

1) When a new line starts with a capital letter, it <u>doesn't</u> mean it's a separate sentence.

2) Just <u>ignore</u> the capitals and follow the <u>punctuation</u>.

3) For example, there's <u>no full stop</u> here so carry on to the next line:

> "This house, these servants and this same myself
> Are yours, my lord: I give them with this ring;"
>
> Act 3, Scene 2

© Donald Cooper/photostage

Look out for words in a funny order

1) Another reason Shakespeare can be <u>tricky</u> to understand is the <u>long complicated sentences</u>.

2) It's hard because the words are in a <u>funny order</u>. If you change the order it makes it <u>easier</u> to understand. For example:

> "And in their ship I am sure Lorenzo is not."
> Act 2, Scene 8

→ And I am sure Lorenzo is not in their ship.

> "Of a strange nature is the suit you follow;"
> Act 4, Scene 1

→ The suit you follow is of a strange nature;

How to Understand Shakespeare's Language

The Merchant of Venice is full of cobwebby, dusty old words and weird ways of writing things using apostrophes. It looks a bit scary, but don't let that put you off — it *is* English really. Definitely. I promise.

You have to guess what the missing letters are

1) Shakespeare often <u>runs two words together</u> and misses letters out to make them fit into a line.

2) There's often an <u>apostrophe</u> instead of the <u>missing letter</u>. So "is't" means "is it".

> "I thank God, I thank God. <u>Is't</u> true, <u>is't</u> true?"
> Act 3, Scene 1

3) If you come across random apostrophes when you're reading, you'll have to <u>work out</u> what the missing letters are.

© Donald Cooper/photostage

Mind your thees, thous and thys

1) They had <u>different words</u> for 'you' in those days.

2) People used to say '<u>thou</u>' to be familiar or friendly, and '<u>you</u>' to be more formal. Look out for these words:

Thou	=	You
Thee	=	You
Thy	=	Your
Thine	=	Your

And finally, some more old, confusing words

1) <u>Verbs</u> often look a bit <u>different</u> from modern English...

thou art	= you are	thou wilt	= you will
thou hast	= you have	thou canst	= you can

2) If this seems difficult, here's a trick — <u>take the 't' off</u> the end of the <u>verb</u>:

hast – t = has
wilt – t = wil(l)

3) Here are a few more words to watch out for:

hie	= go quickly	wherefore	=	why
hither	= to here	thither	=	to there
hence	= from here	whither	=	where
whereof	= of which	ere	=	before

Spend some time getting to grips with the language...

So, Shakespeare missed letters from his words, and he put his words in a funny order. As annoying as that may be, you need to get used to it. The better you understand the play, the better you'll do in your exam.

Analysis of Act One — Antonio Helps a Friend

This section takes you through *The Merchant of Venice* scene by scene. Reading a Shakespeare play is no simple task, but don't panic — these pages will help you to understand all the tricky plot points.

Scene 1 — Antonio is down in the dumps

1) Antonio opens the play by saying "I know not why I am <u>so sad</u>". This creates an oddly <u>downbeat</u> mood for a <u>comedy</u>, which hints that the rest of the play isn't going to be completely <u>light-hearted</u>.

2) Salerio and Solanio assume that Antonio is worried about the <u>safe return</u> of his ships to Venice — "Your mind is <u>tossing on the ocean</u>". This shows that Antonio's business as a merchant is <u>risky</u>.

3) When Antonio <u>denies</u> that he's worried, Salerio thinks that he's <u>in love</u> instead.

4) Antonio's response ("Fie, fie!") <u>denies</u> this too, but it isn't very <u>convincing</u>.

> **Shakespeare's Techniques — Language**
>
> Salerio <u>vividly</u> describes the <u>dangers</u> faced by Antonio's ships. He talks about "<u>roaring waters</u>" and "<u>dangerous rocks</u>", which reinforces the extremely <u>perilous</u> nature of Antonio's business.

5) The real reason behind Antonio's <u>sadness</u> remains a <u>mystery</u> for the rest of the play.

Bassanio asks Antonio for a favour...

1) Bassanio asks Antonio for money. He's desperate to <u>woo Portia</u>, but can't <u>compete financially</u> with her "<u>Renownèd suitors</u>" — he has spent most of his fortune on an <u>expensive lifestyle</u> that he <u>can't afford</u>.

2) The audience questions his <u>motives</u> for wooing Portia. He could want to marry her to "<u>get clear</u>" of his <u>debts</u>.

3) Bassanio's <u>description</u> of Portia doesn't make his motives any <u>clearer</u>. His repetition of "<u>fair</u>" and his praise of her "<u>wondrous virtues</u>" suggests that he does have <u>genuine</u> feelings for her, but a reference to her "<u>worth</u>" shows that he's also thinking about her <u>wealth</u>.

© Moviestore Collection/REX/Shutterstock

... and Antonio agrees

1) Antonio tells Bassanio "my <u>extremest means</u>, / Lie <u>all unlocked</u> to your occasions" <u>before</u> he even knows what Bassanio wants. His <u>eagerness</u> to help Bassanio shows their <u>close friendship</u>.

> **Characters — Antonio and Bassanio**
>
> Act 1, Scene 1 <u>sets the tone</u> for the relationship between Antonio and Bassanio. Antonio's <u>generosity</u> seems <u>excessive</u>, and Bassanio seems <u>reliant</u> on him. For example, Bassanio arguably <u>takes advantage</u> of Antonio's <u>kindness</u> in this scene — he asks him for <u>money</u> even though he's already <u>in debt</u> to him.

2) Antonio gives Bassanio permission to <u>borrow</u> the money <u>in his name</u>. Antonio's use of <u>imperatives</u> such as "<u>go forth</u>; / <u>Try</u> what my credit can in Venice do" shows his <u>determination</u> to help Bassanio.

Consider what each scene reveals about the characters...

First impressions count for a lot — it's no different in a play. The early scenes give you a good idea of what the main characters are like, which provides clues about how they'll behave as the play goes on.

Analysis of Act One — Portia is in Demand

One moment Bassanio is talking about how great Portia is, the next moment the audience gets to meet her for the first time and form their own opinions. It's almost like Shakespeare planned it that way...

Scene 2 — Portia needs a husband...

1) The action jumps to Belmont — a <u>fictional</u> setting in Italy. The pace of this scene is much <u>slower</u> than in Act 1, Scene 1, which creates a <u>calmer atmosphere</u>.

2) Portia's complaint ("my little body is <u>aweary</u> of this great world") echoes Antonio's expression of <u>sadness</u> in Act 1, Scene 1. Unlike Antonio, her sadness is <u>resolved</u> by the end of the play.

3) Portia's father has left a <u>will</u> stating that anyone wanting to marry Portia must choose correctly between a <u>gold casket</u>, a <u>silver casket</u> and a <u>lead casket</u>. Portia disagrees with the casket test — she wants to <u>choose</u> who she marries.

© AF archive / Alamy Stock Photo

Character — Portia's Father

Portia's father is <u>dead</u>, but he still <u>controls</u> who Portia marries using the <u>casket test</u>. In the <u>16th century</u>, it was <u>normal</u> for fathers to <u>decide</u> who their daughters <u>married</u> (see p.38). <u>Shakespeare's audience</u> would probably have thought Portia's father was being <u>caring</u>, but a <u>modern audience</u> might see him as <u>controlling</u>.

4) The scene contains lots of references to Portia feeling <u>restrained</u>. She protests to Nerissa that she can't "<u>choose</u>" or "<u>refuse</u>" any of her suitors, which suggests that she feels <u>trapped</u> by her father's will.

... and there's a long list of suitors

1) Portia recalls the suitors that she has met so far. Her suitors all have <u>different nationalities</u>, which emphasises how <u>sought after</u> Portia is as a wife.

Shakespeare's Techniques — Prose

In this scene, Portia and Nerissa speak in <u>prose</u> (see p.49). This makes their dialogue sound <u>informal</u>, which adds to the <u>relaxed mood</u> of the scene.

2) Portia <u>mocks</u> her suitors using 16th-century <u>national stereotypes</u>. For example, she calls her German suitor a "<u>sponge</u>" (a heavy drinker). Her <u>witty</u> comments create humour and give the scene a <u>light-hearted</u> atmosphere.

3) The audience learns that <u>Bassanio</u> has been to Belmont <u>before</u>. Nerissa says that he deserves "<u>a fair lady</u>", and Portia responds that he's "<u>worthy</u>" of her praise. This hints at Portia later <u>falling in love</u> with Bassanio.

4) The scene <u>ends</u> with the arrival of <u>another suitor</u> — a Moroccan prince. This adds <u>suspense</u>, because it <u>reminds</u> the audience that Bassanio's quest to woo Portia is a <u>race against time</u>.

Character — Portia

Portia may be <u>strong-willed</u> and <u>witty</u>, but she isn't <u>perfect</u>. She <u>hopes</u> the prince doesn't have the "<u>complexion</u> of a <u>devil</u>" (black skin), which reveals an <u>intolerant</u> side to her character that might <u>shock</u> a <u>modern audience</u>.

"I cannot choose one nor refuse none"

Only two scenes in and already the tension is building. Bassanio likes Portia, and there are hints Portia likes him, but she has to marry whoever passes the casket test first. Bassanio had better get a move on...

Analysis of Act One — A Deal is Struck

Bassanio gets hold of the money, but there's an unusual price to pay if the loan isn't repaid in time.

Scene 3 — Bassanio and Antonio approach Shylock

1) Bassanio asks to borrow "three thousand ducats", but Shylock carefully considers his options rather than agreeing straight away. The audience's first impression of him is that he's a shrewd and calculating businessman.

2) This scene introduces the feud between Antonio and Shylock. The tone is tense and confrontational — both characters make accusations against each other and Antonio regularly interrupts Shylock.

3) Shylock reveals that he hates Antonio "for he is a Christian". This presents religion as the main source of their conflict. Their religious differences also cause them to disagree about Shylock's business — Antonio criticises Shylock for charging interest on his loans, but Shylock believes that his trade is justified.

4) Shylock speaks bitterly about the way Antonio has treated him in the past. This gives the audience a conflicted view of Shylock — he's clearly a victim of prejudice, but his drive for revenge makes him seem ruthless.

> **Context — Moneylending**
>
> In 16th-century Venice, Christians thought it was a sin to lend money for profit, but Jews didn't. This explains why Antonio and Shylock disagree about business.

5) The audience also sees a more unpleasant side to Antonio in this scene. Shylock's account of the abuse he has received from Antonio in the past shows that Antonio can be intolerant and cruel.

Shylock makes an odd request

1) Shylock agrees to the loan on the condition that he can have a pound of Antonio's "fair flesh" if it isn't repaid on time. The alliteration of "fair" and "flesh" draws attention to the grisly nature of his request.

2) Shylock's tone is good-natured, but his offer is ominous — he's using the loan as an opportunity to take revenge on Antonio.

3) Bassanio is uncomfortable with the terms, but Antonio's unconcerned attitude makes him seem overconfident — he expects to earn "thrice three times" the amount borrowed when his ships return.

> **Shakespeare's Techniques — Structure**
>
> Shylock draws out Bassanio's request for money by not answering it until near the end of the scene. This shows that he enjoys holding power over the Christians.

> **Shakespeare's Techniques — Dramatic Irony**
>
> Shylock describes the gruesome forfeit as a "merry sport", but the audience knows that he intends to "feed fat" the grudge he holds towards Antonio. Shylock's deception creates dramatic irony and makes him seem villainous.

> Dramatic irony occurs when the audience knows something that the characters don't.

4) Antonio willingly agrees to the terms. This is a significant turning point in the play — Antonio's life now depends on the safe return of his ships.

© Donald Cooper/photostage

> **KEY QUOTE**
>
> ### "My ships come home a month before the day"
>
> To recap, Shylock actually gets to cut a chunk out of Antonio if he can't repay his debt on time.
> Not that it matters, because Antonio's ships are on their way back to Venice as we speak, right...?

Section Two — Discussion of Acts

Analysis of Act Two — A Suitor from Morocco

The scenes come thick and fast in Act 2. It opens with Portia meeting her latest potential husband.

Scene 1 — The prince fancies his chances

1) The Prince of Morocco is <u>proud</u> and <u>imposing</u>. He claims to be loved by the most beautiful women in Morocco and <u>boasts</u> to Portia that he would "<u>outbrave the heart most daring</u> on the earth" to be with her.

© Donald Cooper/photostage

Shakespeare's Techniques — Imagery

The Prince of Morocco uses comparisons to <u>mythological</u> figures like <u>Phoebus</u> and <u>Hercules</u> to make himself seem <u>heroic</u>. The audience's impression of him isn't <u>positive</u>, though — his <u>high opinion</u> of himself makes him seem <u>arrogant</u>.

2) Portia points out that she has been "<u>scanted</u>" (restricted) by her father's <u>dying wishes</u> and has <u>no say</u> in who she marries. Like in Act 1, Scene 2, she emphasises that her fate is <u>out of her hands</u>.

3) The prince asks to be led to the <u>caskets</u>, but Shakespeare doesn't reveal how he gets on until <u>Act 2, Scene 7</u>. This creates <u>suspense</u> for the audience — Bassanio's preparations to leave for Belmont will all have been <u>in vain</u> if the Prince of Morocco <u>passes the test</u>.

Scene 2 — Lancelet finds a new master

1) Lancelet opens the scene with a <u>soliloquy</u> — he's trying to decide if he should <u>stop</u> serving Shylock. His thought process is <u>long</u> and <u>repetitive</u>, which makes him seem <u>foolish</u> and sets a <u>humorous</u> tone for the scene.

> A soliloquy is when a character is alone on stage and speaks their thoughts aloud to the audience.

2) The scene provides <u>light relief</u> — it contains lots of <u>humour</u>:

- Lancelet tricks his blind father (Old Gobbo) into <u>mistaking his identity</u> and thinking that he's <u>dead</u>.
- There's lots of wordplay — Lancelet and Old Gobbo confuse words that <u>sound similar</u>, e.g. "<u>impertinent</u>" and '<u>pertinent</u>'.
- Old Gobbo's wife is called Margery. In Elizabethan <u>slang</u>, this meant '<u>prostitute</u>'.

Shakespeare's Techniques — Humour

The Merchant of Venice is <u>dark</u> for a comedy, so <u>comic</u> scenes are <u>important</u>. It would be <u>boring</u> for the audience if the <u>mood</u> of the play stayed the same <u>throughout</u>.

3) Lancelet uses <u>hyperbole</u> (see p.52) to make <u>Shylock</u> seem <u>stingy</u> and <u>preoccupied</u> with <u>money</u>. He says that he's "<u>famished</u>", which suggests he's <u>underpaid</u> by Shylock. He tells Old Gobbo that he'd rather serve <u>Bassanio</u>, who is <u>generous</u> to his servants.

Shakespeare's Techniques — Poetry and Prose

Lancelet and Old Gobbo speak in <u>prose</u> (see p.48), which shows their <u>low social status</u>. Bassanio speaks in <u>blank verse</u>, which helps to show his <u>higher status</u>.

4) Towards the end of the scene, Bassanio worries that Gratiano is "<u>too wild</u>" and "<u>too rude</u>" to go with him to Belmont. This hints at an <u>unreliable</u> side to Gratiano — one that is later <u>hidden</u> from Nerissa.

EXAM TIP

Make sure you write about the play's structure...

Consider the effect that structure has on the pace of the play. Act 2 has a lot of scenes, and most of them are quite short. This makes it fast-paced, as the action jumps often between different settings and plotlines.

Analysis of Act Two — Jessica Plots Her Escape

Lancelet isn't alone in looking to get away from Shylock — even Shylock's own daughter is at it...

Scene 3 — Jessica is sad to see Lancelet go

1) Jessica says that Lancelet eased the "tediousness" of living with Shylock. Her sadness at the news that Lancelet is leaving tells the audience that she's unhappy at home.

2) With Lancelet gone, Jessica expresses her shame at being Shylock's daughter — "what heinous sin is it in me / To be ashamed to be my father's child!" She feels bound to him by blood, but nothing more.

Character — Jessica

Jessica's feelings of shame are linked to Shylock's Jewish identity — she doesn't consider herself to be Jewish, but is still labelled as a Jew through association with her father. The only way for Jessica to distance herself from her Jewish heritage is to reject Shylock.

3) She intends to run away with Lorenzo and become a Christian by marrying him. Her main motive for doing this is to "end this strife". This suggests she may only be converting to Christianity to escape from her Jewish background, not because she truly wants to convert.

Scene 4 — Lorenzo gets a letter

1) Lorenzo and his companions are preparing to attend a masque (a fancy-dress ball) when he receives a letter containing Jessica's escape plan. Lorenzo recognises Jessica's "fair hand" instantly, which hints at the strength of his feelings for her.

2) Jessica plans to steal her father's "gold and jewels" before disguising herself as Lorenzo's torchbearer to escape. The mention of theft makes Jessica's abandonment of Shylock seem more heartless.

© Manuel Harlan

Scene 5 — Shylock heads out for the evening

1) Shylock is reluctant to dine with Bassanio. He worries that there's "some ill a-brewing", and is even less willing to go when he hears there's going to be a masque. His concerns give the scene a sinister mood.

2) Shylock leaves Jessica in charge, telling her to "stop my house's ears" against the celebrations. This personification shows Shylock's desire to shut out the sound of the masque from his "sober house."

Character — Shylock

Shylock's clear dislike of the Christian celebrations in this scene reinforces Jessica's claim that he's 'tedious' (boring) to live with.

3) As Shylock leaves, Jessica says "if my fortune be not crost, / I have a father, you a daughter, lost." In other words, she'll be gone before Shylock returns if her escape goes to plan. This rhyming couplet gives Jessica's speech a decisive tone, which emphasises how determined she is to leave.

EXAM TIP

Explain how the audience might feel about Shylock...

Think about how the audience's opinion of Shylock changes. He isn't the most sympathetic character in Act 1, but Jessica's betrayal in Act 2 makes it more possible for the audience to feel sorry for him.

Analysis of Act Two — The Caskets are Revealed

The plan goes smoothly and the lovers are united. Sadly, the Prince of Morocco isn't quite so lucky...

Scene 6 — Jessica makes her escape

1) At the start of the scene, Gratiano and Salerio discuss <u>love</u>. Gratiano remarks that "All things that are, / <u>Are with more spirit chasèd than enjoyed</u>" — to him, the <u>pursuit</u> of love is much more exciting than successfully <u>finding</u> it.

Character — Gratiano

Gratiano's comment hardly makes him seem like an <u>ideal husband</u>. It doesn't <u>bode well</u> for his relationship with <u>Nerissa</u> if he finds the <u>chase</u> the <u>most exciting</u> part.

2) Gratiano and Salerio make multiple references to <u>time</u>. When Gratiano says that Lorenzo "out-dwells his hour", he suggests that time is <u>running out</u> for the escape to go ahead. This creates a <u>tense atmosphere</u>.

3) This scene is the <u>first time</u> the audience sees Jessica and Lorenzo on stage <u>together</u>. Their relationship seems <u>heartfelt</u> — Jessica calls Lorenzo "<u>my love</u>" and Lorenzo <u>affectionately</u> calls Jessica "<u>sweet</u>".

4) The scene ends with news that <u>Bassanio</u> is about to <u>sail</u> for Belmont, which creates <u>anticipation</u>.

Scene 7 — The Prince of Morocco chooses poorly

1) The audience <u>finally</u> sees someone take the casket test, <u>eight scenes</u> after it was introduced. Portia tells the prince he can marry her if he picks the one containing her <u>picture</u>. Each one has its own <u>inscription</u>:

- The <u>gold</u> casket reads "Who chooseth me shall gain <u>what many men desire</u>."
- The <u>silver</u> casket reads "Who chooseth me shall get <u>as much as he deserves</u>."
- The <u>lead</u> casket reads "Who chooseth me must <u>give</u> and <u>hazard all he hath</u>."

The symbolism of the casket test is discussed on p.51.

© Donald Cooper/photostage

2) The Prince of Morocco picks the <u>gold</u> casket. He chooses according to what Portia and the casket itself <u>look like</u> — he uses a <u>metaphor</u> to describe Portia, saying she's "so rich a <u>gem</u>" that it would be "<u>sinful</u>" to put a picture of her in any other casket.

3) Inside the gold casket is a poem, which criticises the prince for basing his decision on <u>outward appearance</u> alone — "<u>All that glitters is not gold</u>". This suggests that looks can be <u>deceiving</u>, which is a <u>recurring</u> idea in the play (see p.40-41).

4) After he <u>fails</u> the test, the prince doesn't say much to Portia before he <u>leaves</u> the stage. His <u>subdued</u> manner contrasts with his <u>confidence</u> in Act 2, Scene 1 and shows how <u>upset</u> he is.

Theme — Appearance and Reality

The Prince of Morocco learns the <u>hard way</u> that judging by outward appearances is a <u>bad idea</u>. He picks the <u>gold</u> casket for <u>superficial</u> reasons and leaves Belmont <u>empty-handed</u> as a result.

5) Portia feels <u>relieved</u> — "Let all of his complexion choose me so." Her comment reveals that she <u>judges</u> the prince by the <u>colour of his skin</u>. This suggests <u>outward appearances</u> matter to her too.

KEY QUOTE *"I have too grieved a heart / To take a tedious leave"*

He's a little on the pompous side, but that doesn't necessarily make the Prince of Morocco a bad person — in fact, he's gracious in defeat. He certainly doesn't deserve the prejudice Portia shows towards him.

Analysis of Act Two — A Suitor from Aragon

Portia's in luck as another suitor fails the test, but things are about to take an ominous turn for Antonio.

Scene 8 — Shylock is fuming...

1) The audience first hears about Shylock's <u>reaction</u> to Jessica's <u>betrayal</u> through Salerio and Solanio. This <u>distances</u> the audience from Shylock's character, which makes it easier for him to be <u>ridiculed</u>.

2) Solanio <u>mimics</u> Shylock crying "<u>My daughter! O my ducats!</u>" Switching between "daughter" and "ducats" makes it unclear which loss has <u>upset</u> Shylock more — <u>Jessica</u> or his <u>money</u>.

3) Shylock's <u>foul mood</u> makes Solanio <u>afraid</u> of what might happen to Antonio if he <u>can't repay</u> his loan. His <u>fear</u> sets a <u>sinister</u> tone which lasts for the rest of the scene.

> **Character — Shylock**
>
> Other characters often talk <u>negatively</u> about Shylock when he isn't on stage. Salerio and Solanio's <u>mockery</u> is meant to be <u>funny</u>, but a <u>modern audience</u> might feel <u>sorry</u> for Shylock instead.

... and there's worrying news for Antonio

1) Salerio has been told that a ship has <u>run aground</u> in the English Channel — it <u>may</u> be one of Antonio's. The uncertainty over this <u>rumour</u> creates <u>tension</u>, because the audience <u>doesn't know</u> what to believe.

2) Salerio and Solanio agree to break the news to Antonio <u>gently</u>. This shows their <u>close friendship</u> with Antonio — they don't <u>want</u> to upset him.

3) Salerio's description of Antonio in this scene is full of <u>admiration</u> ("A <u>kinder gentleman</u> treads not the earth"). Flattering descriptions like this one <u>idealise</u> Antonio, which makes it easier for the audience to view him as Shylock's <u>victim</u>.

> **Characters — Antonio and Bassanio**
>
> Antonio and Bassanio <u>aren't</u> present in this scene, but the audience <u>learns</u> more about their <u>relationship</u> from Salerio and Solanio. When Solanio says that Antonio "<u>only loves the world</u>" because of Bassanio, it makes the <u>depth</u> of Antonio's love for Bassanio <u>stand out</u>.

Scene 9 — The Prince of Aragon tries his luck with the caskets

1) This scene <u>echoes</u> the action of Act 2, Scene 7. The Prince of Aragon is shown the caskets, presents the reason for his choice, but ultimately <u>fails</u>. This highlights the <u>flaws</u> shared by both of the princes.

© Donald Cooper/photostage

2) The Prince of Aragon <u>avoids</u> joining the "<u>fool multitude</u>" who would choose the <u>gold</u> casket for its <u>appearance</u>, but his reason for choosing the <u>silver</u> casket is also <u>vain</u>. He <u>arrogantly</u> assumes that he <u>deserves</u> Portia.

3) The <u>poem</u> in the silver casket tells the prince that he has chosen <u>foolishly</u>. He clearly <u>doesn't learn</u> anything from his failure, as he insists that the outcome is "<u>unlike</u>" his "<u>deservings</u>" — he's just as <u>arrogant</u> as he was before.

4) Act 2 ends with word of a "<u>young Venetian</u>" arriving at Belmont. This hints that <u>Bassanio</u> has come at last. Ending the scene <u>here</u> leaves the audience in <u>suspense</u>.

Learn some useful quotes to back up your points...

All of the best exam answers are packed with relevant quotes to support their arguments. Using quotes shows that you know the play really well and gives you the chance to do some close language analysis.

Analysis of Act Three — Mixed News for Shylock

Shylock's having a hard time, but he perks up when he hears that Antonio's in a bit of bother too.

Scene 1 — Shylock is still angry...

1) Salerio has heard another <u>rumour</u> that a ship has <u>run aground</u> off the coast of England — it seems <u>certain</u> that it belongs to Antonio. This creates an <u>ominous</u> mood at the start of Act 3.

2) Shylock accuses <u>Salerio</u> and <u>Solanio</u> of being involved in Jessica's "<u>flight</u>". They use <u>wordplay</u> to <u>taunt</u> Shylock — Salerio says that he knows who "<u>made the wings</u>", while Solanio suggests that Jessica was "<u>fledged</u>" (ready to fly the nest). Their <u>mocking</u> tone shows that they have <u>no sympathy</u> for Shylock.

3) In this scene, the audience witnesses Shylock's anger <u>first hand</u>. He says that Jessica is "<u>damned</u>", which shows he thinks her decision to <u>abandon</u> her father and her faith has <u>condemned</u> her soul.

4) Jessica's betrayal <u>strengthens</u> Shylock's desire to see Antonio <u>suffer</u>. He tries to justify his <u>vengeful</u> attitude:

- He recalls how Antonio has always treated him <u>unfairly</u>. Antonio has "<u>disgraced</u>", "<u>mocked</u>" and "<u>scorned</u>" him because he's a Jew.

- He argues that Jews are <u>no different</u> to Christians using a series of <u>rhetorical questions</u> — "Hath not a Jew eyes?", "If you tickle us, do we not laugh?" and "If you poison us, do we not die?"

- Shylock points out that it's only <u>natural</u> for him to seek revenge, as that's exactly what a <u>Christian</u> would do in the <u>same situation</u>.

Character — Shylock

Shylock's speech is <u>powerful</u> — his <u>language</u> is <u>persuasive</u> and his points are <u>convincing</u>. By highlighting his <u>humanity</u>, Shylock shows that he's just as <u>deserving</u> of <u>sympathy</u> as Antonio.

... and he finds out what Jessica's been up to

1) Salerio and Solanio are <u>summoned</u> to Antonio's house, leaving Shylock to speak with his <u>friend</u>, Tubal.

Theme — Wealth

The ring is <u>valuable</u> to Shylock for <u>sentimental</u> reasons. He's still concerned about his <u>money</u>, but he <u>proves</u> that money isn't <u>all that matters</u> to him when he tells Tubal he wouldn't have traded the ring for a "<u>wilderness of monkeys</u>".

© Donald Cooper/photostage

2) Tubal returns from Genoa after being sent to look for <u>Jessica</u>. He has heard that she's <u>recklessly</u> spending Shylock's money and has even traded his precious <u>ring</u> for a <u>monkey</u>. Shylock is <u>most upset</u> by the loss of the ring, which was given to him by Leah (his <u>dead wife</u>).

3) Tubal has also heard that another of Antonio's ships has been <u>wrecked</u>. He says that Antonio is "<u>undone</u>" — this creates a sense of <u>foreboding</u> as the audience realises that Antonio will be <u>unable to repay</u> his debt.

4) Shylock is "<u>very glad</u>" to hear of Antonio's <u>ill luck</u> and immediately sends Tubal to make plans for his <u>arrest</u>. His <u>swift</u> reaction suggests that he'll show <u>no mercy</u>.

5) The audience sees two <u>extremes</u> to Shylock's character in this scene — he seems <u>victimised</u>, but also <u>spiteful</u>. This leads the audience to <u>question</u> whether or not his status as the <u>villain</u> of the play is completely <u>justified</u>.

"if you wrong us, shall we not revenge?"

Shylock's big speech in Act 3, Scene 1 is an important moment in the play. There's no longer any doubt in the audience's mind that Shylock means business — it seems like he'll stop at nothing to have his revenge.

Analysis of Act Three — Bassanio Chooses Wisely

Bassanio isn't hanging about — he wins Portia, but before you know it, he's on a boat back to Venice.

Scene 2 — Bassanio passes the test of the caskets...

1) Portia <u>encourages</u> Bassanio to "<u>pause</u> a day or two" before <u>taking</u> the casket test. She's <u>worried</u> that he'll choose <u>incorrectly</u> and be forced to leave. Her <u>anxiety</u> reveals the strength of her <u>feelings</u> for Bassanio.

2) Bassanio is <u>eager</u> to take the test. He says "For as I am, I live upon the <u>rack</u>" — not knowing whether he can marry Portia is like <u>torture</u> to him.

3) Unlike the princes of Morocco and Aragon, Bassanio recognises that appearances can be <u>misleading</u> and correctly chooses the <u>lead casket</u>.

Theme — Appearance and Reality

Bassanio reveals a <u>flaw</u> in the test of the caskets. He <u>wins</u> Portia, but he isn't the <u>honourable</u> man her father had hoped for. He <u>deceives</u> others by pretending to be <u>wealthy</u>, which is why he understands that <u>appearances</u> can be <u>misleading</u>.

© Nigel Norrington / ArenaPAL

4) Portia gives Bassanio a <u>ring</u>, and tells him that to <u>lose</u> it would signify the "<u>ruin</u>" of his love for her. Her <u>warning</u> becomes more <u>significant</u> in Act 4, when she <u>tricks</u> Bassanio into giving the ring <u>away</u>.

5) Portia and Bassanio are almost overcome with <u>happiness</u>. Gratiano and Nerissa announce their own <u>engagement</u>, which adds to the <u>joyful mood</u>.

...but his happiness is short-lived

1) Bassanio receives a <u>letter</u> from Antonio containing "a few of the <u>unpleasant'st words</u> / That ever blotted paper" — <u>none</u> of Antonio's ships have <u>returned</u> to Venice. The news that Antonio's life is in danger marks a <u>turning point</u> in the mood of the scene — it suddenly becomes <u>more serious</u>.

2) Salerio's report creates <u>tension</u> by making Antonio's death seem <u>inevitable</u> — Shylock is <u>ignoring</u> pleas for <u>mercy</u> from some of the most important men in Venice. This suggests he is <u>determined</u> to see Antonio <u>suffer</u>.

Theme — Justice and Mercy

The Christian characters repeatedly try to <u>persuade</u> Shylock to show <u>mercy</u> to Antonio, but they <u>don't</u> succeed. Shylock seems more <u>ruthless</u> each time he insists on <u>justice</u> in the form of a <u>pound of flesh</u>.

3) Even though Portia has never met Antonio, she offers to pay <u>whatever it takes</u> to save his life. She sees it as her duty as Bassanio's wife to help his "<u>dearest friend</u>".

4) Bassanio leaves as <u>soon</u> as he can. His <u>hasty departure</u> shows how <u>loyal</u> he is to Antonio — their <u>friendship</u> is so <u>important</u> to Bassanio that he leaves Portia on their <u>wedding night</u>.

Shakespeare's Techniques — Structure

Shakespeare <u>structures</u> this scene so that Bassanio's <u>loyalty</u> to Antonio <u>overshadows</u> his <u>love</u> for Portia. The letter <u>draws</u> the audience's attention <u>away</u> from Bassanio and Portia's engagement, and Antonio's fate becomes the <u>main focus</u> of the action. The wedding <u>doesn't even feature</u> in the scene.

EXAM TIP

Think about Bassanio's conflicting loyalties...

Even though Bassanio and Portia have just got engaged, Bassanio has to return to Venice to help Antonio. It's worth considering how his loyalties are divided and the problems this causes later on in the play.

Analysis of Act Three — Portia Hatches a Plan

Revenge is in sight for Shylock and he has no intention of letting it slip. Antonio could do with some help...

Scene 3 — Antonio pleads with Shylock

1) Shylock meets Antonio, who has been <u>arrested</u>. Antonio seems <u>vulnerable</u> in this scene. The way he <u>pleads</u> with Shylock to "<u>hear me speak</u>" shows the audience of how <u>powerless</u> he has become.

2) Shylock repeats the phrase "<u>I'll have my bond</u>". This shows that his <u>grudge</u> towards Antonio is now an <u>obsession</u> — he's become so focused on revenge that he can think of <u>nothing else</u>.

> **Context — Venice**
>
> In the 16th century, Venice's <u>prosperity</u> depended on <u>trade</u>. The Duke can't deny Shylock his bond in case it causes traders to <u>lose faith</u> in his ability to <u>uphold</u> the <u>laws</u> of the city. If they did, there's a <u>good chance</u> they'd take their business <u>elsewhere</u>.

3) Solanio hopes the Duke of Venice might <u>intervene</u>, but Antonio explains that even the Duke "<u>cannot deny the course of law</u>".

4) Antonio is <u>resigned</u> to his fate — he just wants to <u>see Bassanio</u> before he <u>dies</u>. The fact that Bassanio is the <u>only</u> character mentioned by Antonio suggests that he's the one Antonio <u>cares</u> about <u>most</u>.

5) Antonio doesn't <u>fully understand</u> why Shylock wants him <u>dead</u>. He thinks that Shylock <u>hates</u> him for <u>paying</u> off other people's debts, but doesn't consider that <u>abusing</u> Shylock in the <u>past</u> might be another reason. This could imply that Antonio still <u>doesn't believe</u> the way he treated Shylock was <u>unreasonable</u>.

Scene 4 — Portia's up to something...

1) Lorenzo speaks highly of Antonio, calling him a "<u>gentleman</u>" and a <u>loving friend</u>. His <u>compliments</u> echo Bassanio's <u>praise</u> in Act 3, Scene 2 and encourage the audience to feel <u>sympathy</u> for Antonio's situation.

2) Portia tells Lorenzo that using her <u>own</u> money to rescue Antonio is a <u>small price</u> to pay if he's as good a <u>friend</u> as people say. This makes Portia seem <u>selfless</u>.

3) Portia <u>lies</u> to Lorenzo. She convinces him that she and Nerissa will wait for their husbands in a <u>nearby monastery</u>, but <u>secretly</u> makes plans to go to <u>Venice</u>.

> **Character — Portia**
>
> Portia <u>obeys</u> her father's dying wishes and <u>submits</u> her <u>authority</u> to Bassanio in Act 3, Scene 2. However, this scene shows her <u>manipulating</u> a male character. This suggests that she isn't always as <u>passive</u> and <u>submissive</u> as a 16th-century woman was <u>expected</u> to be.

© ERREBI/REX/Shutterstock

4) Portia tells her <u>servant</u> to take a <u>letter</u> to <u>Doctor Bellario</u> (her cousin in Padua), then meet her by the <u>ferry</u> to Venice. She asks him to do it with "<u>imagined speed</u>" (as quickly as possible), which adds to the <u>tension</u> by suggesting that time is <u>running out</u> to save Antonio's life.

In the 16th century, the word 'doctor' was also used to refer to lawyers.

KEY QUOTE

"since I am a dog, beware my fangs"

What goes around comes around. In Act 1, Scene 3, the audience finds out that Antonio called Shylock a "cut-throat dog". The insult clearly stuck with Shylock, as he refers back to it in Act 3 to threaten Antonio.

Analysis of Act Three — A Little Light Relief

You can always rely on Lancelet to provide some much-needed humour when the going gets tough.

... but it isn't clear what

1) Portia tells Nerissa she has a <u>plan</u>, but doesn't give away many details. She <u>vaguely</u> states that "I have work in hand / <u>That you yet know not of</u>". The way she <u>conceals</u> information creates <u>suspense</u>, because the audience <u>doesn't know</u> what she's planning yet.

2) When Portia tells Nerissa that they will be <u>disguising</u> themselves as men, she <u>mocks</u> men for their habits. She demonstrates an <u>in-depth</u> knowledge of how men <u>behave</u>, which could help to explain why her disguise as a male lawyer is so <u>convincing</u> later on.

© Donald Cooper/photostage

3) The audience has to <u>wait</u> until Act 4, Scene 1 to see exactly <u>why</u> Portia and Nerissa need disguises. This makes Portia's appearance in the <u>courtroom</u> more <u>dramatic</u>, because the audience <u>doesn't</u> see it coming.

Scene 5 — Lancelet is a nuisance

1) Lancelet tells Jessica that she's "<u>damned</u>" for her Jewish origins, because "<u>the sins of the father</u> are to be <u>laid upon the children</u>". He thinks that Jessica will <u>never</u> be able to <u>escape</u> her Jewish background.

2) Jessica replies that "I shall be <u>saved</u> by my husband; he hath <u>made me a Christian</u>." Her tone is <u>confident</u>, but Lancelet's comment puts her acceptance as a Christian <u>in doubt</u>.

3) Lancelet jokes that converting <u>Jews</u> into <u>Christians</u> (or "<u>pork-eaters</u>") would <u>raise</u> the price of pork for everyone else. His <u>light-hearted</u> tone makes the mood of the scene less <u>serious</u>.

> Many Jews don't eat pork for religious reasons.

4) Lancelet <u>irritates</u> Lorenzo by deliberately <u>misinterpreting</u> his instructions. His behaviour here is <u>similar</u> to his behaviour in Act 2, Scene 2, when he tricks Old Gobbo. This highlights Lancelet's role as a <u>mischief-maker</u> in the play — he often creates <u>confusion</u> for others.

Shakespeare's Techniques — Puns and Wordplay

In this scene, Shakespeare uses words with <u>double meanings</u> to create <u>comedy</u>. When Lorenzo orders Lancelet to have the servants "<u>prepare for dinner</u>", Lancelet comments that the servants are always prepared for dinner as "<u>they have all stomachs</u>". Lorenzo's <u>exasperation</u> entertains the audience.

Character — Portia

Jessica greatly <u>admires</u> Portia, even though she doesn't <u>know</u> her very well. Many of the other characters also <u>praise</u> Portia <u>highly</u>, which contributes to her <u>positive image</u> in the play.

5) Lorenzo questions Jessica about Portia. Jessica clearly has a <u>high opinion</u> of her, as she thinks that Bassanio is <u>blessed</u> to have her in his life.

6) Lorenzo remarks that Jessica is <u>equally lucky</u> to have a husband like him — Jessica isn't so sure. Their <u>playful</u> conversation makes their <u>relationship</u> seem <u>affectionate</u>.

EXAM TIP

Give examples of how Shakespeare lightens the mood...

The play's longest and most dramatic scene is up next, so it's hardly surprising that Shakespeare wanted to get a few laughs in first. Act 3, Scene 5 eases the tension so that it can be built back up again in Act 4.

Analysis of Act Four — Antonio's Trial Begins

The whole play has been building up to this moment — Shylock finally gets his opportunity for revenge.

Scene 1 — The law is on Shylock's side...

1) Antonio is brought before the Duke and other influential figures in Venice ("the Magnificoes"). Their presence highlights the importance of the scene and creates anticipation in the audience. The setting (a court of justice) also makes the scene quite serious.

2) Antonio knows that "no lawful means" can save him. His only hope is for Shylock to take pity on him.

3) The Duke's sympathy clearly lies with Antonio, as he asks Shylock to show mercy. He's shocked that Shylock actually plans to take Antonio's flesh, but Shylock is outraged at the idea of being denied it.

... and Shylock knows it

1) The Duke is in a difficult situation. He wants to save Antonio, but knows that he would have to break the law to do it. Shylock recognises this. He's so confident of success that he admits he's only acting out of "a certain loathing" for Antonio.

© AF archive / Alamy Stock Photo

2) Bassanio offers Shylock six thousand ducats (twice what Antonio owes), but Shylock refuses them. This confirms that the money isn't as important to him now — the main thing he cares about is revenge.

3) Antonio tells Bassanio to give up and let him die. His resigned tone makes the mood even more sombre.

Portia's plan is revealed

1) Just as the Duke reveals that he's expecting Doctor Bellario to come, Nerissa enters disguised as a lawyer's assistant. She says that Doctor Bellario has sent a lawyer called Balthasar (who is actually Portia) in his place. Portia's arrival gives the audience renewed hope that Antonio's life will be saved.

2) Portia delivers a speech on the "quality of mercy" which is full of religious imagery. She argues that to show mercy is to act like "God himself". This presents mercy as an important Christian value.

> **Character — Doctor Bellario**
>
> Doctor Bellario doesn't appear in person in the play, but the disguises he provides are crucial to the plot. They allow Portia to intervene in the trial, as women weren't allowed to practise law in the 16th century.

3) Shylock scorns Portia's speech and tells her "I crave the law, / The penalty and forfeit of my bond." His insistence on justice is his downfall, as the wording of his bond is the loophole that Portia later exploits.

4) Bassanio feels desperate — he offers to pay Shylock ten times the sum he's owed "On forfeit of my hands, my head, my heart". In contrast, Shylock is delighted that the trial seems to be going his way, calling Portia a "wise and upright judge". These contrasting emotions make the scene more dramatic.

KEY QUOTE

"How shalt thou hope for mercy, rendering none?"

The Duke's question foreshadows the dramatic turnaround that's about to take place. At the time, Shylock says he has no need for mercy, but he'll soon regret his answer when he finds himself in Antonio's shoes.

Section Two — Discussion of Acts

Analysis of Act Four — Portia Outwits Shylock

Just when it seems like Antonio is done for, Portia cleverly turns the wording of the bond to her advantage.

Antonio is saved...

1) The drama <u>peaks</u> as Portia tells Antonio to "<u>lay bare</u>" his chest. Shylock now appears particularly <u>villainous</u> — he even has a set of <u>scales</u> ready to weigh Antonio's flesh.

2) As Shylock goes to cut Antonio, Portia tells him to "<u>Tarry a little</u>". She informs him that as he's entitled to <u>exactly</u> "a pound of <u>flesh</u>", he can't take <u>any</u> of Antonio's <u>blood</u>. This is a <u>turning point</u> in Shylock's fortunes — he realises his bond is <u>worthless</u>, because it's <u>impossible</u> to claim it without spilling <u>blood</u>.

3) Portia stresses the <u>importance</u> of mercy <u>earlier</u> in the scene, but <u>doesn't</u> ask the Duke to show Shylock any mercy. This <u>confirms</u> Shylock's belief that the Christians aren't as <u>merciful</u> as they think (see p.37).

4) Unlike Portia, the Duke is <u>merciful</u>. He <u>spares</u> Shylock's life, telling him that it should help him "<u>see the difference of our spirits</u>". However, Shylock doesn't go <u>unpunished</u>:

© United Archives GmbH / Alamy Stock Photo

- He's told to surrender <u>half</u> of his wealth to Antonio, who will <u>pass it on</u> to Lorenzo and Jessica when Shylock <u>dies</u>.
- He's allowed to <u>keep</u> the other half for the moment, but has to leave <u>everything</u> to Lorenzo and Jessica in his <u>will</u>.
- He's forced to <u>convert</u> to Christianity.

5) These punishments are <u>devastating</u> for Shylock. His <u>religious beliefs</u> are central to his <u>identity</u>, but he has to <u>give them up</u>. To add insult to injury, the man who took away his daughter will inherit <u>everything</u> he owns.

... but his saviour needs rewarding

1) Antonio and Bassanio <u>thank</u> the lawyer, <u>unaware</u> that it's Portia. <u>Dramatic irony</u> creates <u>humour</u> here — Bassanio offers Portia the <u>money</u> that she herself gave to him in Act 3, Scene 2.

2) Portia asks for Bassanio's <u>ring</u> as a <u>test of his loyalty</u>. Bassanio resists, but Antonio <u>persuades</u> him to give it away.

3) The <u>conclusion</u> of Act 4, Scene 1 signals an end to the play's <u>tragic</u> elements. The two remaining scenes are much more <u>light-hearted</u>.

Character — Antonio

Antonio's actions <u>undermine</u> Portia. When he tells Bassanio to measure the <u>value</u> of their <u>friendship</u> against the <u>value</u> of his <u>promise</u> to Portia, he suggests Bassanio's commitment to his wife is <u>less important</u>.

Scene 2 — Nerissa decides to test Gratiano's loyalty

1) Shylock's fate <u>isn't mentioned again</u> after this point — this helps Shakespeare give the play a <u>happy ending</u>.

2) Like Portia, Nerissa tests her husband's <u>loyalty</u>. She tries to get Gratiano to part with his ring <u>as well</u>. This shows a <u>similarity</u> between Portia and Nerissa — both of them are <u>keen</u> to teach their husbands a <u>lesson</u>.

KEY QUOTE

"Thou shalt have justice, more than thou desirest"

Portia plays with Shylock's expectations — she leads him to believe that he's getting what he wants before snatching his hopes away. The only justice he'll be getting is for attempted murder of a Venetian citizen...

Analysis of Act Five — Bassanio is Fooled

After the drama and intensity of Act 4, Act 5 brings the play to a light-hearted close.

Scene 1 — Portia and Nerissa return to Belmont...

1) Lorenzo and Jessica declare their love for one another by comparing themselves to couples from Greek myths, like <u>Troilus and Cressida</u> and <u>Thisbe and Pyramus</u>.

> **Shakespeare's Techniques — Imagery**
>
> Lorenzo and Jessica speak to each other like <u>lovers</u>, but make some <u>odd</u> comparisons. Cressida <u>betrays</u> Troilus, while Thisbe and Pyramus both <u>commit suicide</u>. By referencing couples with <u>tragic endings</u>, Shakespeare hints that Lorenzo and Jessica's relationship won't end well either.

See p.50 for more on Shakespeare's use of imagery.

2) Shakespeare creates a <u>serene atmosphere</u> with a combination of "<u>sweet music</u>" and <u>natural imagery</u>. This reflects the shift from the <u>drama</u> of the court scene to the more <u>romantic focus</u> of the final scene.

3) Portia warns Lorenzo and Jessica not to mention her <u>absence</u> from Belmont to Bassanio — she needs Bassanio and Gratiano to remain <u>ignorant</u> of the lawyer's <u>true identity</u> for the <u>practical joke</u> to work.

... and make fools of their husbands

1) When Bassanio arrives, he compares Portia to the <u>sun</u>. This echoes the <u>natural imagery</u> used by Lorenzo to describe the <u>night sky</u>, which maintains the <u>romantic mood</u> established at the beginning of the scene.

2) Portia and Nerissa tell their husbands off for <u>giving away</u> their rings. In this part of the scene, <u>dramatic irony</u> creates <u>humour</u> — the audience <u>enjoys</u> watching Bassanio and Gratiano try to <u>defend themselves</u>.

3) The women eventually <u>reveal</u> that they have the rings, but they suggest that they got them back by being <u>unfaithful</u>. In the 16th century, it was very <u>humiliating</u> for a man to have an <u>unfaithful wife</u>. If true, Portia and Nerissa's claims would <u>disgrace</u> their husbands.

© Nigel Norrington / ArenaPAL

4) Portia reveals that she was the <u>lawyer</u> and Nerissa was her <u>assistant</u>. The men are <u>astounded</u> — they had <u>no idea</u> that their wives were in the <u>courtroom</u>.

> **Theme — Appearance and Reality**
>
> Bassanio isn't <u>always</u> taken in by <u>outward appearances</u> — if he was, he <u>wouldn't</u> have passed the casket test back in Act 3, Scene 2. However, he's <u>unable</u> to see through Portia's <u>disguise</u>. This shows that he isn't as <u>perceptive</u> as the outcome of the casket test suggests.

5) The play ends on a <u>jubilant</u> note with even more <u>good news</u> from Portia. She tells Antonio that three of his ships have <u>returned</u> to Venice, and lets Lorenzo know he'll <u>inherit</u> Shylock's <u>fortune</u>.

6) In <u>typical fashion</u> for a comedy, the couples are <u>happily reconciled</u>. However, Antonio remains <u>alone</u>. This hints that he might not <u>love women</u> in the same way as the other male characters.

EXAM TIP

Talk about the mythological imagery in the play...

Shakespeare uses a lot of mythological imagery in the play (see p.50). No one's asking you to be an expert in Greek mythology, but your answers will really stand out if you can explain what he's getting at.

Practice Questions

You've done the hard bit by making it through this section, so you might as well round it off by answering all these questions. You shouldn't need more than a sentence or two to answer the Quick Questions, and your answers to the In-depth Questions should be about a paragraph long. Nothing too demanding to see here...

Quick Questions

1) Why does Bassanio ask Antonio for money?

2) How does the casket test work?

3) What must Antonio do if he can't repay his debt to Shylock on time?

4) Why are the rumours that Salerio and Solanio discuss bad news for Antonio?

5) Why is Shylock particularly upset when he hears Jessica has traded his ring for a monkey?

6) What item does Portia give Bassanio as a symbol of their love in Act 3, Scene 2?

7) Where does Portia go after she tells Lorenzo that she'll wait for Bassanio in a monastery?

8) Who is Doctor Bellario?

9) Why can't Shylock take Antonio's flesh in Act 4, Scene 1?

10) What punishments are given to Shylock for trying to kill Antonio?

In-depth Questions

1) Which of the following moments marks the biggest turn in Shylock's fortunes? Explain why.
   a) Antonio borrows money from him   b) Jessica abandons him   c) Portia outwits him

2) Do you think Bassanio is a good friend to Antonio?
   Back up your points using examples from the play.

3) How does Portia treat Bassanio differently to the way she treats her other suitors?

4) Do you think Jessica's betrayal of Shylock is justified? Explain your answer.

5) Explain how a light-hearted atmosphere is created in Act 5, Scene 1.

Practice Questions

Now that you're all warmed up, it's time for some Exam-style Questions. You might find some of them a bit tricky, but it could be worse — you could have a vengeful moneylender trying to cut you into teensy pieces...

Exam-style Questions

1) Read the extract below, then answer the questions.

Portia:	You, merchant, have you anything to say?
Antonio:	But little: I am armed and well prepared.
	Give me your hand, Bassanio: fare you well!
	Grieve not that I am fallen to this for you;
	For herein Fortune shows herself more kind
	Than is her custom: it is still her use
	To let the wretched man outlive his wealth,
	To view with hollow eye and wrinkled brow
	An age of poverty; from which lingering penance
	Of such misery doth she cut me off.
	Commend me to your honourable wife:
	Tell her the process of Antonio's end;
	Say how I loved you, speak me fair in death;
	And, when the tale is told, bid her be judge
	Whether Bassanio had not once a love.
	Repent not you that you shall lose your friend,
	And he repents not that he pays your debt;
	For if the Jew do cut but deep enough,
	I'll pay it presently with all my heart.
Bassanio:	Antonio, I am married to a wife
	Which is as dear to me as life itself;
	But life itself, my wife, and all the world,
	Are not with me esteemed above thy life:
	I would lose all, ay, sacrifice them all
	Here to this devil, to deliver you.

(Act 4, Scene 1)

a) How is the relationship between Antonio and Bassanio presented in this extract?

b) In this extract, Antonio keeps his agreement with Shylock and accepts his fate. Explore the importance of obedience elsewhere in the play. You should consider:
- which characters are obedient
- how obedience is important to the play.

2) Read Act 5, Scene 1 from "**What ring gave you my lord?**" to "**some woman had the ring**." Explain the importance of loyalty in this extract and elsewhere in the play.

3) Read Act 3, Scene 2 from "**You see me, Lord Bassanio**" to "**my vantage to exclaim on you**." Discuss how Shakespeare presents different ideas about money in the play. You should refer to the extract and the play as a whole in your answer.

4) Read Act 3, Scene 2 from "**I pray you, tarry**" to "**as treason and my love**." How does Shakespeare present the relationship between Bassanio and Portia in this extract and the rest of the play?

Character Profile — Antonio

You need to know the characters inside out if you want to write good essays, so now it's time for a much closer look at them. First up is Antonio, a rich merchant who finds himself in a bit of bother...

Antonio is popular and respected

1) Antonio is a <u>wealthy</u> and <u>successful</u> merchant.

2) His <u>good reputation</u> in business means that it's <u>easy</u> for him to borrow the money that Bassanio needs.

3) His friends greatly <u>admire</u> him — Salerio says that "A <u>kinder</u> gentleman treads not the earth." They're <u>concerned</u> when he's upset and do everything they can to <u>help him</u> when he's in trouble with Shylock.

Shakespeare's Techniques — Hyperbole

Salerio is <u>exaggerating</u> for effect when he says "A kinder gentleman treads not the earth" — this is an example of <u>hyperbole</u>. It emphasises Antonio's <u>extreme generosity</u>.

4) Despite his <u>success</u> and <u>popularity</u>, Antonio is a <u>sad</u> character. The <u>source</u> of his misery isn't revealed, and he's an <u>outsider</u> among three <u>happy couples</u> at the end of the play.

He's generous to Bassanio...

1) When Bassanio asks Antonio for money to help him <u>woo</u> Portia, Antonio <u>doesn't hesitate</u> to give him as much as he needs.

2) Antonio is also willing to <u>die</u> for Bassanio once it becomes clear that he <u>won't</u> be able to <u>repay</u> his debt to Shylock.

Antonio is...

melancholy: "In sooth, I know not why I am so sad"

selfless: "Grieve not that I am fallen to this for you"

prejudiced: "The Hebrew will turn Christian: he grows kind."

3) Antonio's <u>generosity</u> can be seen as a <u>flaw</u>. He's so <u>keen</u> to help Bassanio that he <u>foolishly endangers</u> his own life. Bassanio <u>warns</u> him that agreeing to Shylock's terms is a <u>bad idea</u>, but Antonio <u>doesn't listen</u>.

... but prejudiced towards Shylock

1) Antonio hates Shylock simply because he's <u>Jewish</u>. Shylock reveals in Act 1, Scene 3 that Antonio has <u>spat on him</u>, <u>kicked him</u> and called him a "<u>cut-throat dog</u>" and "<u>misbeliever</u>".

2) Antonio <u>can't see</u> the damage his <u>prejudice</u> causes. He doesn't <u>recognise</u> that the <u>harsh</u> way he has treated Shylock in the past is part of the <u>reason</u> Shylock wants to get <u>revenge</u> on him.

3) Although he's cruel to Shylock, Antonio still appears as the <u>victim</u>. His <u>subdued</u> acceptance of his fate contrasts with Shylock's <u>frenzied</u> desire for <u>revenge</u>.

The vicious side to Antonio's character doesn't bother the other Christians — this suggests that they share his prejudiced views.

4) Antonio's reason for forcing Shylock to <u>convert</u> to Christianity <u>isn't clear</u> — he may want to take <u>revenge</u> on Shylock, but it's also possible that he believes he's offering him <u>salvation</u> (see p.37).

Explain Antonio's role in his own misfortune...

Shakespeare wants the audience to feel sympathy for Antonio — he's only trying to do the right thing by helping out a friend. That said, it's worth considering his own role in making Shylock resent him.

Character Profile — Bassanio

Antonio and Bassanio go together like tea and biscuits, so it's only fair that Bassanio should be up next.

Bassanio is well liked...

1) Bassanio is Antonio's <u>closest friend</u> — Solanio says that Antonio "<u>only loves the world for him</u>".

2) Bassanio's <u>cheerful</u> and <u>courteous</u> nature makes him a very <u>likeable</u> character, particularly in the eyes of Portia and Nerissa — they both remember him <u>fondly</u> from a visit he made to Belmont <u>in the past</u>.

© Elliot Franks / ArenaPAL

3) He's also a bit of a <u>risk-taker</u>, meaning he's <u>perfectly suited</u> to succeed at the test of the caskets. He's the only suitor who's willing to "<u>hazard all he hath</u>" to win Portia, which is why he picks the <u>lead</u> casket.

Bassanio is...

friendly: "Good signiors both, when shall we laugh?"

impulsive: "I will be bound to pay it ten times o'er,
On forfeit of my hands, my head, my heart"

romantic: "Madam, you have bereft me of all words"

... and extremely loyal

1) Bassanio is <u>uncomfortable</u> with the <u>terms</u> of Shylock's loan — he tells Antonio that "you <u>shall not</u> seal to such a bond for me". He wants the money to <u>woo Portia</u>, but he cares <u>more</u> about Antonio's <u>wellbeing</u>.

2) He rushes back to Venice as soon as he hears that Antonio's <u>in trouble</u>, and even offers to <u>sacrifice himself</u> in Antonio's place — "The Jew shall have my <u>flesh</u>, <u>blood</u>, <u>bones</u> and <u>all</u>".

3) Bassanio is also loyal to his <u>wife</u>. He's initially <u>reluctant</u> to part with <u>Portia's ring</u>, saying that he would rather give away the "<u>dearest ring</u> in Venice". He does eventually give in, but only <u>under pressure</u> from Antonio.

Theme — Love

At the end of Act 4, Scene 1, Bassanio's <u>loyalties</u> are torn. He has to choose between his <u>friendship</u> with Antonio and his <u>marriage</u> to Portia. When he gives his ring away, Bassanio appears to prioritise Antonio over Portia, which creates <u>conflict</u> in the play's final scene.

He can be reckless and selfish

1) Bassanio <u>isn't perfect</u>. He's <u>unable</u> to support himself <u>financially</u> due to his <u>careless spending</u> in the past.

2) He <u>takes advantage</u> of Antonio's <u>generosity</u> by asking for money when he's already in his <u>debt</u>. He knows borrowing money is a <u>risk</u> for Antonio ("Thou know'st that <u>all my fortunes are at sea</u>"), but <u>asks anyway</u>.

3) Bassanio's <u>motivations</u> for marrying Portia aren't all <u>romantic</u>. He certainly <u>loves</u> Portia, but he's also conscious of how "<u>richly left</u>" she is and sees marrying her as a chance to make his <u>fortune</u>.

Write about Bassanio's good and bad qualities...

Bassanio's quite a contradictory character. He may be well liked and loyal, but he's also partly to blame for getting Antonio into trouble. He also appears to love Portia's money almost as much as he loves her.

Character Profile — Portia

Intelligence, wealth, beauty — Portia's got it all. No wonder Bassanio's so keen on marrying her...

Portia is highly sought after

1) Portia's <u>wealth</u> and <u>beauty</u> make her very <u>desirable</u> as a wife — her suitors come from <u>all over</u> the world.

2) However, being <u>desired</u> doesn't make Portia <u>happy</u>. In Act 1, Scene 2, she feels "<u>curbed</u>" by her father's wishes and <u>dreads</u> marrying someone she <u>doesn't like</u>.

3) Portia could <u>disobey</u> her father's will by telling Bassanio which casket to choose, but decides not to. This shows that respecting her father is <u>more important</u> to her than her own <u>happiness</u>.

© Donald Cooper/photostage

Go back to p.14 to refresh your memory on the test of the caskets.

Portia is...

quick-witted: "we'll outface them, and outswear them too."

humble: "This comes too near the praising of myself; / Therefore no more of it"

scornful: "God made him, and therefore let him pass for a man."

She's intelligent and opinionated...

1) Portia is the <u>heroine</u> of the play. She saves Antonio's life by cleverly <u>outwitting</u> Shylock — she leads him to insist on the <u>exact wording</u> of his bond, then turns his <u>own words</u> against him.

Theme — Justice and Mercy

Portia tells Shylock that he "shall have merely <u>justice</u> and his <u>bond</u>". She knows Shylock can't take a pound of Antonio's flesh without spilling <u>any blood</u> — this puts Shylock in an <u>impossible situation</u>.

2) Women were expected to be <u>obedient</u> to their husbands in the 16th century, but Portia <u>defies</u> these expectations. She asserts her <u>authority</u> over Bassanio by <u>tricking</u> him.

3) Portia is very <u>opinionated</u>. She's <u>polite</u> to her suitors in person, but judges them <u>harshly</u> in private. Her <u>opinions</u> can also be <u>prejudiced</u> (see p.43).

... but also has a softer side

1) The audience sees <u>another side</u> to Portia when Bassanio first arrives at Belmont — she's <u>affectionate</u> and <u>submissive</u>. This contrasts with the <u>polite</u> but <u>distant</u> way she treats the princes of Morocco and Aragon.

Shakespeare's Techniques — Language

In Act 3, Scene 2, Portia tells Bassanio that "One half of me is <u>yours</u>, the other half <u>yours</u>". The <u>repetition</u> of "yours" shows she's ready to <u>devote</u> herself to Bassanio <u>completely</u>.

2) Portia is a <u>virtuous</u> character. She has <u>strong morals</u> and tries to do what she thinks is <u>right</u>. She <u>selflessly</u> intervenes in Antonio's trial and tries to teach Shylock the <u>importance of mercy</u>.

3) Portia isn't as <u>cruel</u> to Shylock as she could be. She gives him <u>several</u> chances to "<u>tear the bond</u>" (drop his case against Antonio) and <u>walk away</u> with the money.

KEY QUOTE

"I never did repent for doing good, / Nor shall not now"

Portia's actions are the source of a lot of happiness in the play — she saves Antonio's life and secures a sizeable inheritance for Lorenzo and Jessica. All in all, she's quite a handy person to have around...

Character Profile — Shylock

Even comedies often have a bad guy, and *The Merchant of Venice* is no different. Enter Shylock...

Shylock is often seen as a villain

1) In Act 1, Shakespeare introduces Shylock as a <u>greedy</u> moneylender with a <u>bloodthirsty</u> desire for <u>revenge</u>.

2) The way other characters <u>talk about</u> Shylock adds to the audience's <u>negative</u> impression of him — Jessica says their house is "<u>hell</u>" and the Christian characters often refer to Shylock as the "<u>devil</u>" (see p.50).

3) Shylock's Jewish <u>identity</u> is an important part of his image as a <u>villain</u> and <u>outsider</u>. He's <u>outnumbered</u> by Christians who <u>despise</u> him for his faith, and his lifestyle excludes him from <u>cultural activities</u>, like the <u>masque</u> (Act 2, Scene 5).

Context — Jews in Venice

In the 16th century, there was lots of <u>hostility</u> between <u>Jews</u> and <u>Christians</u> (see p.43). Jews were <u>allowed</u> to live in Venice because they had an <u>important</u> role in the <u>economy</u>, but they weren't fully <u>accepted</u> into society. Shylock's <u>treatment</u> by the Christians would probably have been quite <u>normal</u> at the time.

He's a vengeful character...

1) Shylock is <u>out to get</u> Antonio from the <u>start</u>. In Act 1, Scene 3, he reveals that he holds an "<u>ancient grudge</u>" against Antonio.

2) Shylock's desire for <u>revenge</u> grows <u>stronger</u> when Jessica runs away with Lorenzo — a Christian. His <u>grief</u> and <u>fury</u> at being <u>betrayed</u> make him more determined to see Antonio <u>suffer</u>.

3) He repeatedly <u>dismisses</u> pleas to spare Antonio's life — "<u>tell not me of mercy</u>". He believes that taking a pound of Antonio's flesh is the <u>only</u> way he'll have <u>justice</u> for the way Antonio has treated him in the past.

4) Shylock's <u>obsession</u> with revenge is eventually his <u>downfall</u> in the court scene. He has several chances to take the money and leave, but ends up <u>losing everything</u> and being forced to <u>convert to Christianity</u>.

Shylock is...

prejudiced: "I hate him for he is a Christian"

stubborn: "I'll have my bond"

ill-treated: "sufferance is the badge of all our tribe."

... but he's not a complete monster

1) Shylock is <u>victimised</u> for his <u>faith</u> — this could make a <u>modern audience</u> feel <u>sorry</u> for him (see p.43).

© Donald Cooper/photostage

2) Shylock's lengthy speech to Salerio in Act 3, Scene 1 highlights how <u>unfairly</u> he's treated by showing that he's every bit as <u>human</u> as the <u>Christian characters</u>.

3) Shylock is <u>devastated</u> when Tubal tells him that Jessica has sold a turquoise <u>ring</u> given to Shylock by his wife — "Thou <u>torturest</u> me, Tubal". His <u>emotional</u> response shows a more <u>tender</u> side to his character.

4) Shylock <u>doesn't appear</u> in the final act, and the other characters already seem to have <u>forgotten</u> about him. This might make an audience <u>today</u> wonder if he really <u>deserved</u> his <u>harsh punishments</u> at the <u>trial</u>.

KEY QUOTE

"Cursèd be my tribe, / If I forgive him!"

Shylock is sick and tired of being treated unfairly by the play's Christian characters. He's presented with a chance to get his own back, and feels like it would be an insult to other persecuted Jews if he didn't take it.

Character Profile — Jessica

Jessica has it tough, but she's no innocent bystander — she's got a ruthless streak, just like her dad...

Jessica can be seen as a victim...

© Moviestore Collection/REX/Shutterstock

1) Jessica <u>hates</u> living with Shylock. The <u>only time</u> the audience sees them at home together is in Act 2, Scene 5. Shylock uses lots of <u>imperatives</u>, e.g. "<u>Do as I bid you</u>", which makes the atmosphere seem <u>oppressive</u>.

2) Jessica admits that she's "<u>ashamed</u>" to be Shylock's daughter. The audience feels <u>sympathy</u> for her <u>internal conflict</u> — she doesn't want to be <u>Jewish</u>, but knows it is a "<u>heinous sin</u>" to reject her <u>family origins</u>.

3) Marrying Lorenzo <u>doesn't</u> solve all of Jessica's <u>problems</u>. After the couples come back to Belmont in Act 5, Jessica doesn't speak again. This could suggest she hasn't been fully <u>accepted</u> into <u>Christian society</u>.

Jessica is...

independent: "though I am daughter to his blood, / I am not to his manners."

determined: "I have a father, you a daughter, lost."

insensitive: "Here, catch this casket; it is worth the pains."

... but she isn't totally innocent

1) Jessica <u>betrays</u> Shylock's <u>trust</u> when she <u>abandons</u> him and <u>steals</u> from him. She <u>doesn't care</u> if her actions <u>hurt</u> Shylock, which makes her seem <u>selfish</u>.

Jessica's cruelty makes it easier to sympathise with Shylock's character.

2) She spends the stolen money <u>wastefully</u> and trades Shylock's ring "<u>for a monkey</u>". This suggests that she didn't need the money in the first place, and that she might be <u>deliberately</u> trying to <u>upset</u> Shylock.

3) When the other characters return to Belmont in Act 5, Scene 1, Jessica <u>doesn't react</u> to the news of Shylock's fate. Lorenzo is <u>delighted</u> when he hears about their inheritance, but Jessica stays <u>silent</u>. This leaves the audience wondering how she's feeling — she shows neither <u>concern</u> nor <u>happiness</u>.

Her motives for marriage are unclear

1) When Lorenzo comes to help Jessica escape from Shylock, she speaks to him using <u>romantic language</u>. This suggests that she <u>does have</u> feelings for Lorenzo.

2) However, Shakespeare hints that Lorenzo isn't <u>perfect</u> for Jessica — she <u>doesn't agree</u> with Lorenzo's speech about "<u>the sweet power of music</u>" in Act 5, Scene 1.

Shakespeare's Techniques — Language

In Act 2, Scene 6, Jessica's dialogue with Lorenzo is full of <u>romantic imagery</u>. She refers to "<u>Cupid</u>" — the Roman god of desire. This makes their relationship seem <u>passionate</u>.

3) This makes the audience <u>question</u> if Jessica marries Lorenzo <u>purely</u> out of <u>love</u>. She might also marry him to <u>get away</u> from Shylock. Her motives for <u>converting</u> to Christianity are <u>equally unclear</u> — the audience can't tell if she does it to <u>escape</u> her Jewish heritage, or if she <u>truly</u> wants to be a Christian.

EXAM TIP

Consider both sides to Jessica's character...

The idea that appearances can be misleading doesn't only apply to the caskets — it includes characters too. It's easy to feel sorry for Jessica, but don't forget that the way she treats her father is quite cruel.

Character Profile — Nerissa

Every Batman needs a Robin — Portia's the heroine, but she wouldn't get far without her sidekick Nerissa.

Nerissa is a voice of reason

1) Nerissa is Portia's <u>lady-in-waiting</u> and <u>close friend</u>.

2) When she's introduced in Act 1, Scene 2, several of her lines sound like <u>proverbs</u> — <u>popular sayings</u> that express a <u>common truth</u>. This makes her seem <u>wise</u>.

3) As Portia's parents are <u>dead</u>, Nerissa is her main source of <u>advice</u>. She reminds Portia that her "<u>good fortunes</u>" outweigh her "<u>miseries</u>" and reassures her that she'll find a <u>worthy</u> husband.

> A lady-in-waiting is a companion, not a servant. Nerissa has a lower status than Portia, but she's also from a noble family.

Nerissa is...

intelligent: "they are as sick that surfeit with too much as they that starve with nothing."

perceptive: "Bassanio, lord Love, if thy will it be!"

playful: "the doctor's clerk, / In lieu of this last night did lie with me."

She's very close to Portia...

1) Nerissa shows her <u>dedication</u> to Portia by <u>disguising</u> herself as the lawyer's clerk to help her save Antonio.

2) Nerissa puts <u>Portia's happiness</u> before her own. She won't get married unless Portia does too, and checks that Portia <u>approves</u> of her match <u>before</u> agreeing to it.

3) The <u>only</u> time that Nerissa and Portia speak in <u>prose</u> is to each other in Act 1, Scene 2. This suggests that they are <u>comfortable</u> with each other.

© Moviestore Collection/REX/Shutterstock

4) Nerissa and Portia's <u>close relationship</u> is emphasised by the way that Nerissa <u>mirrors</u> Portia's character — they both <u>find husbands</u> in Act 3, Scene 2, and both <u>trick their partners</u> into giving away their rings.

... and demands loyalty from Gratiano

1) Nerissa's <u>relationship</u> with Gratiano reveals <u>more</u> about her <u>personality</u> — she's <u>playful</u> and <u>determined</u>.

2) She <u>gains control</u> in the relationship by <u>tricking</u> him. She gets him to <u>give away</u> the ring he had earlier sworn to "<u>keep for ever</u>", before telling him off for <u>supposedly</u> giving it to <u>another woman</u>.

3) During the play, Nerissa doesn't show much <u>emotion</u>. This makes her <u>outburst</u> to Gratiano in Act 5, Scene 1 ("What talk you of the posy or the value?") more <u>powerful</u>.

Shakespeare's Techniques — Mood and Atmosphere

When Nerissa <u>criticises</u> Gratiano for giving away his ring and claims to have <u>cuckolded</u> him, she provides some much needed <u>comic relief</u> for the audience. This contributes to the <u>light-hearted</u> atmosphere of Act 5, Scene 1.

> In Elizabethan times, a cuckold was a man who had an unfaithful wife.

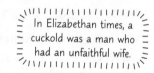

"good joy: good joy, my lord and lady!"

Everyone could do with a friend like Nerissa in their life — she's always rooting for Portia and great fun to be around. That said, it looks like Gratiano needs to be on his best behaviour now he's married to her.

Character Profile — Lorenzo and Gratiano

Lorenzo and Gratiano aren't the sharpest tools in the shed, but they've got some redeeming qualities...

Lorenzo is head over heels for Jessica

1) Lorenzo is a <u>Christian</u> who is <u>in love</u> with Jessica. He's one of the most <u>romantic</u> characters in the play — he talks <u>openly</u> about his <u>feelings</u> for Jessica and discusses the <u>beauty</u> of <u>music</u>.

2) Lorenzo can be <u>reckless</u>. He <u>runs away</u> with Jessica, but he doesn't have a <u>clear plan</u> for their <u>future</u> — their stay at <u>Belmont</u> hints that they've got <u>nowhere</u> to live.

3) At the end of the play, Lorenzo is very <u>grateful</u> for the money he'll <u>inherit</u> from Shylock, but there's <u>little</u> to suggest he won't <u>waste</u> that too. He describes himself and Jessica as "<u>starvèd people</u>", which implies that the money <u>stolen</u> from Shylock is already <u>all gone</u>.

> **Lorenzo is...**
>
> **passionate:** "How sweet the moonlight sleeps upon this bank!"
>
> **sincere:** "You have a noble and a true conceit Of godlike amity"

© Donald Cooper/photostage

> **Theme — Prejudice**
>
> Lorenzo's <u>love</u> and <u>respect</u> for Jessica makes him seem less <u>prejudiced</u> than some of the play's other Christian characters. However, he's not completely <u>open-minded</u>. For example, he still refers to Shylock as a "<u>faithless Jew</u>".

Gratiano is an energetic character

1) Gratiano is <u>friends</u> with the other Venetian men, but he's particularly <u>close</u> to <u>Bassanio</u>. He goes with Bassanio to Belmont, where he <u>marries</u> Nerissa.

2) Gratiano doesn't take life very <u>seriously</u>. His <u>energy</u> contrasts with Antonio's <u>sadness</u> in Act 1, Scene 1, when he lectures Antonio on the importance of "<u>mirth and laughter</u>".

3) He's a bit of a <u>liability</u> — Bassanio describes Gratiano's behaviour as "<u>wild</u>" and fears it could <u>hurt</u> his chances of marrying Portia if Gratiano comes to Belmont.

4) Gratiano's relationship with Nerissa <u>mirrors</u> Bassanio's relationship with Portia from Act 3, Scene 2 onwards. Both undergo a <u>test of loyalty</u> and have a <u>happy ending</u>.

5) However, Gratiano <u>doesn't</u> show Nerissa the same amount of <u>affection</u> that Bassanio shows Portia — this suggests that his love might not be as <u>strong</u>.

6) Act 4, Scene 1 reveals a <u>sinister</u> side to Gratiano's character. He says that Shylock "must be <u>hanged</u>" and tells him "<u>be thou damned</u>, inexecrable dog!" The <u>dark</u> and <u>violent</u> imagery that Gratiano uses illustrates his <u>ruthless</u> attitude towards Jews.

> **Shakespeare's Techniques — Language**
>
> The <u>repetitive structure</u> of Gratiano's lines "<u>You</u> saw the mistress, <u>I</u> beheld the maid; / <u>You</u> loved, <u>I</u> loved" reflects the <u>similarities</u> between Gratiano and Bassanio's romantic relationships.

> **Gratiano is...**
>
> **outspoken:** "too wild, too rude and bold of voice"
>
> **spontaneous:** "My eyes, my lord, can look as swift as yours"

"lovers ever run before the clock"

In Act 2, Scene 6, Gratiano comments on how rashly people act when they're in love. He's not wrong, either — Lorenzo steals Jessica from Shylock, while Gratiano himself marries a woman he's only just met.

Character Profile — Other Characters

Just when you thought it was safe to turn the page, there's a bunch of minor characters to bear in mind too. Not to worry, though — read these pages and it'll soon be time for a well-earned break.

Salerio and Solanio keep the audience informed

1) Salerio and Solanio are <u>friends</u> to Antonio, Bassanio, Gratiano and Lorenzo.

2) Their actions have a <u>limited impact</u> on the plot. They are mainly used as <u>narrative devices</u>, which means that they communicate <u>important events</u> that happen <u>off stage</u> to the audience:

- In Act 2, Scene 8, they give a <u>brief account</u> of Shylock's <u>immediate reaction</u> to Jessica's <u>betrayal</u>.
- In Act 3, Scene 1, they discuss a <u>rumour</u> that one of Antonio's ships has <u>run aground</u> near England.
- In Act 3, Scene 2, Salerio travels to <u>Belmont</u> to inform <u>Bassanio</u> of Antonio's <u>misfortune</u>.

3) Salerio is <u>perceptive</u> — he's one of the <u>first</u> to hear the <u>rumours</u> about Antonio's ships and he understands their <u>implications</u> for Antonio. Solanio is <u>more naive</u> — he thinks the <u>Duke</u> will stop Shylock from <u>harming</u> Antonio.

4) Both Salerio and Solanio are <u>loyal</u> to Antonio. In Act 1, Scene 1, they are <u>concerned</u> to see that Antonio is "<u>so sad</u>". As the play goes on, Solanio <u>stays</u> with Antonio and <u>comforts</u> him — "the duke / Will <u>never grant this forfeiture</u>".

© Donald Cooper/photostage

Lancelet's main role is to provide comedy

1) Lancelet is the play's <u>clown</u> character. He starts out as a servant to <u>Shylock</u>, but later serves <u>Bassanio</u>.

2) He is the only <u>recurring</u> character who always speaks in <u>prose</u> (see p.48), which sets him apart from the play's other characters — it highlights his <u>lower status</u> as a servant.

3) He doesn't have many <u>close relationships</u> — the <u>only</u> character he seems to care about is <u>Jessica</u>. He's <u>visibly sad</u> to leave her in Act 2, Scene 3 and agrees to act as a <u>go-between</u> for her and Lorenzo.

Theme — Prejudice

In spite of his close relationship with Jessica, Lancelet is still an anti-Semitic (<u>anti-Jewish</u>) character. During Act 2, Scene 3, he suggests that only a Christian could make someone as "<u>beautiful</u>" and "<u>sweet</u>" as Jessica.

Shakespeare's Techniques — Mood and Atmosphere

Lancelet's scenes don't always contribute to the <u>overall plot</u>, but his character helps the <u>tension</u> to <u>rise and fall</u> instead of constantly keeping the audience in <u>suspense</u>. Dramatic moments <u>lose</u> their impact if they happen in <u>every scene</u>.

4) He's <u>mischievous</u> — he <u>tricks</u> his blind father into thinking he's <u>dead</u> (Act 2, Scene 2) and <u>deliberately</u> annoys Lorenzo (Act 3, Scene 5).

5) Lancelet often <u>confuses</u> similar-sounding words, like "<u>reproach</u>" (abuse) instead of '<u>approach</u>' (arrival) and — another sign of his low status and lack of <u>education</u>.

6) These <u>malapropisms</u> (<u>unintentional</u> uses of <u>wrong</u> words) create <u>humour</u>, as other characters respond to what they <u>hear</u> as opposed to what Lancelet really <u>means</u>.

Character Profile — Other Characters

The Duke holds authority in Venice

1) As the most <u>influential</u> man in Venice, the Duke has the <u>power</u> to decide Antonio's fate <u>in court</u>.

2) The Duke should be <u>impartial</u>, but he makes it <u>obvious</u> from the start of Act 4, Scene 1 that he's <u>on Antonio's side</u> — he tells Antonio he's "<u>sorry</u>" for him and calls Shylock an "<u>inhuman wretch</u>".

Theme — Justice and Mercy

In spite of his <u>clear preference</u> for Antonio, the Duke won't <u>bend the rules</u> in his favour. Denying Shylock his bond would damage Venice's <u>reputation</u> for upholding the law.

3) The Duke <u>spares</u> Shylock's life. His <u>merciful attitude</u> sets him apart from the other Christians. He also doesn't let <u>anger</u> or <u>revenge</u> alter his <u>principles</u>, which makes him seem <u>honourable</u>.

4) However, he still agrees to some <u>harsh punishments</u>, like Shylock's <u>conversion</u> to Christianity.

The Prince of Morocco is arrogant...

1) The Prince of Morocco is a <u>boastful</u> character. In Act 2, Scene 1, he <u>brags</u> to Portia about his <u>good looks</u> and <u>military prowess</u>.

2) He chooses the <u>gold</u> casket because he sees Portia as a <u>precious</u> "gem" that shouldn't be placed in anything "<u>worse than gold</u>". The scroll in the casket <u>criticises</u> him for basing his decision on <u>outward appearances</u>, and he's made to look like a <u>fool</u> for having been so <u>confident of success</u>.

© Donald Cooper/photostage

Theme — Appearance and Reality

Shakespeare highlights the Prince of Morocco's preoccupation with appearances in Act 2, Scene 1. The "*Flourish of cornets*" gives his arrival a sense of <u>grandeur</u> and his speech is full of <u>elaborate</u> imagery, which makes it more <u>memorable</u>.

3) He isn't a totally <u>unsympathetic</u> character, though. He's <u>gracious</u> in <u>defeat</u> and doesn't deserve the <u>prejudice</u> Portia shows towards him.

... much like the Prince of Aragon

1) The Prince of Aragon only has <u>one short scene</u> to leave an <u>impression</u> on the audience.

2) He's presented as <u>self-important</u> — he considers himself <u>better</u> than the "<u>barbarous multitudes</u>" who would pick the <u>gold</u> casket, and chooses the <u>silver</u> casket because he feels <u>entitled</u> to Portia.

3) The Prince of Aragon's <u>disbelief</u> at failing the test of the caskets shows his <u>arrogance</u> — "How much unlike my hopes and my deservings!" In spite of the outcome of the test, he still believes he <u>deserves</u> to marry Portia.

Thanks to the Prince of Aragon, the audience knows which casket is the right one for Bassanio to choose.

EXAM TIP

Don't forget about the minor characters...

Shakespeare didn't just throw characters into his plays at random — everyone's included for a reason. The characters on these pages may not seem as important, but you still need to learn about them.

Practice Questions

As if learning the characters' names wasn't hard enough, you also need to learn what they're like, how they feel about each other, what they do and why they do it. Luckily, these questions are a great way of checking that it's all sunk in. Why not reward yourself for answering them all with a trip to Venice? Or, you know, a cup of tea...

Quick Questions

1) Which three words best describe Antonio?
   a) discontent   b) generous   c) tolerant   d) melancholy   e) greedy

2) Which aspect of Bassanio's personality makes him well-suited to succeed at the casket test?

3) Why is Portia unhappy in Act 1, Scene 2?

4) What is the name of Portia's lady-in-waiting?

5) Give two moments in the play when the audience might feel sorry for Shylock.

6) Which of these relationships mirrors Bassanio and Portia's relationship most closely?
   a) Gratiano and Nerissa   b) Lorenzo and Jessica   c) Salerio and Solanio

7) Who is the play's clown character?

8) How does the Duke's behaviour in Act 4, Scene 1 set him apart from the other Christians?

In-depth Questions

1) Explain why Antonio and Shylock dislike each other so much.
   Use quotes from the play to support your answer.

2) Do you think Bassanio marries Portia for love or money?
   Back up your answer using evidence from the play.

3) How does Shakespeare show that Portia and Nerissa are close in the play?

4) Does Shylock deserve his punishments in Act 4, Scene 1? Explain your answer.

5) Do you think Lorenzo and Jessica make a good couple?
   Explain why / why not, using examples from the play.

6) Explain the role of Salerio and Solanio in the play.

Practice Questions

Time to take it up a notch. The following questions are exactly the sort of thing that you can expect to see in the exam. They're not easy, but putting in a bit of extra time and effort now will do wonders when it comes to tackling the real thing. If you get stuck on what to write, flick back through the section for some ideas.

Exam-style Questions

1) Read the extract, then answer the questions below.

Shylock:	How now, Tubal! What news from Genoa? Hast thou found my daughter?
Tubal:	I often came where I did hear of her, but cannot find her.
Shylock:	Why, there, there, there, there! A diamond gone, cost me two thousand ducats in Frankfurt! The curse never fell upon our nation till now; I never felt it till now: two thousand ducats in that; and other precious, precious jewels. I would my daughter were dead at my foot, and the jewels in her ear! Would she were hearsed at my foot, and the ducats in her coffin! No news of them? Why, so: and I know not what's spent in the search: why, thou loss upon loss! The thief gone with so much, and so much to find the thief; and no satisfaction, no revenge: nor no ill luck stirring but what lights on my shoulders; no sighs but of my breathing; no tears but of my shedding.
Tubal:	Yes, other men have ill luck too: Antonio, as I heard in Genoa —
Shylock:	What, what, what? Ill luck, ill luck?
Tubal:	— hath an argosy cast away, coming from Tripolis.
Shylock:	I thank God, I thank God. Is't true, is't true?
Tubal:	I spoke with some of the sailors that escaped the wreck.
Shylock:	I thank thee, good Tubal: good news, good news! Ha, ha, heard in Genoa?

(Act 3, Scene 1)

    a) How is Shylock's state of mind presented in this extract?

    b) How does Shakespeare present revenge in the play?

2) Read the whole of Act 2, Scene 3. How is the relationship between Jessica and Shylock portrayed in this extract and elsewhere in the play?

3) Read Act 2, Scene 8 from "**Marry, well remembered**" to the end of the scene. How does Shakespeare present Antonio in this extract and elsewhere in the play?

4) To what extent can Shylock be seen as the villain of the play?

Justice and Mercy

Justice and mercy are two of the most important themes in *The Merchant of Venice*. They can also be a bit tricky to understand, so read these pages carefully if you want to do yourself justice in the exam...

Not everyone views justice in the same way

© Donald Cooper/photostage

1) Justice means different things to different characters. Shakespeare explores this idea using the quarrel between Antonio and Shylock.

2) The Christian characters can't understand why Shylock doesn't drop his case against Antonio — they think paying off Antonio's debt should give Shylock justice, but Shylock disagrees.

3) Shylock's view of justice is different. He has suffered abuse from Antonio for a long time and sees the bond as an opportunity to make Antonio suffer in return — "The villainy you teach me, I will execute".

4) These different attitudes towards justice can be found in the two main sections of the Bible — the Old Testament and the New Testament:

In the Old Testament...	In the New Testament...
... justice works on the principle that the penalty for any crime must be just as severe as the crime itself. This idea is similar to the vengeful attitude that Shylock adopts throughout the play.	... Christians are encouraged to show forgiveness to those who wrong them. This is the merciful attitude the Christian characters want Shylock to show Antonio.

The Jewish Scriptures are made up of the books of the Old Testament, while the New Testament only appears in the Bible. Many Jews today disagree with the harsh views on punishment in their Scriptures.

5) These contrasting views on justice make it impossible for the court case between Antonio and Shylock to be resolved fairly. Whatever the outcome, one of them will see the result as unjust.

The law initially gives Shylock confidence...

1) 16th-century Venice was an independent state, which meant that it made its own laws. These promoted fairness and equality for all — the courtroom is the only place where Shylock believes he can get justice, despite being Jewish.

2) The law gives Shylock power over the Christian characters. He reminds the Duke that he can't deny him his bond, saying that to do so would violate the "freedom" he's meant to protect.

> **Character — Shylock**
> Shylock allows himself to become overconfident. This makes his change in fortune in Act 4, Scene 1 more dramatic, because he doesn't see it coming.

3) The Christian characters recognise that Shylock has the upper hand. When Bassanio asks Portia to bend the rules for Antonio, she tells him that "no power in Venice / Can alter a decree establishèd". This makes it seem inevitable that the court will rule in Shylock's favour, which adds to the tension.

... but his confidence is misplaced

1) Portia undermines Shylock's faith in the law by turning it against him in Act 4, Scene 1. When she tells him he can't take Antonio's blood, he asks "Is that the law?" His question shows his surprise.

2) In legal terms, Shylock does receive justice — it's just not the justice that he thinks he's entitled to.

3) His preoccupation with revenge and his stubborn refusal to show mercy to Antonio ultimately result in his downfall. This shows that the law isn't an effective means of justice for everyone.

Justice and Mercy

The Christians urge Shylock to show mercy...

1) The play's <u>Christian</u> characters strongly believe in <u>showing mercy</u> to others
— they encourage Shylock to be <u>merciful</u> to Antonio throughout the play.

2) Portia's "<u>quality of mercy</u>" speech in Act 4, Scene 1 <u>powerfully defends</u> the idea of mercy. She tells Shylock that pursuing revenge will <u>condemn</u> his soul — only showing mercy can bring him <u>salvation</u>.

3) In Elizabethan England, seeking <u>revenge</u> went against <u>Christian morals</u>. Shakespeare's audiences were mainly <u>Christian</u>, so they wouldn't have agreed with Shylock's <u>vengeful attitude</u>.

... but aren't always merciful themselves

1) Shylock <u>mocks</u> the Christian view of mercy. In Act 4, Scene 1, he <u>accuses</u> the Christian characters of being <u>hypocrites</u>. He points out that Christians purchase <u>slaves</u> and put them to work like "<u>asses</u>" and "<u>dogs</u>". They buy <u>human flesh</u> and do as they please with it, so Shylock thinks he can too.

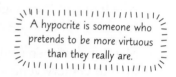

A hypocrite is someone who pretends to be more virtuous than they really are.

2) Shylock's <u>accusation</u> is <u>proved right</u> when he's <u>punished</u> at the end of Antonio's trial:

- Portia lectures Shylock on the <u>importance of mercy</u> when <u>Antonio's life</u> is at risk, but makes <u>no appeal</u> to the Duke when <u>Shylock's life</u> is in danger.

- Gratiano <u>criticises</u> Shylock for his <u>vengeful attitude</u> during the trial. Despite this, he wants <u>revenge</u> on Shylock at the end of the trial — he says that he "<u>must be hanged</u>".

3) However, the Christian characters <u>genuinely</u> believe that they're <u>merciful</u> to Shylock. The Duke <u>spares</u> his <u>life</u> to show "the <u>difference of our spirits</u>" and Portia asks Antonio "What <u>mercy</u> can you render him"?

4) A <u>modern</u> audience is <u>less likely</u> to think that the Christians characters are <u>merciful</u> to Shylock— they wouldn't view forcing someone to <u>give up</u> their <u>religion</u> as <u>acceptable</u>.

Not everyone gets what they deserve

1) The <u>harshness</u> of Shylock's <u>punishments</u> leads the audience to <u>question</u> whether he really <u>deserves</u> them. He's <u>relentless</u> in seeking revenge, but only because he's received so much <u>abuse</u> in the <u>past</u>.

© Donald Cooper/photostage

Context — Christian Beliefs

Shylock's <u>forced conversion</u> isn't necessarily <u>intended</u> to be so harsh. 16th-century Christians believed that Jews went to <u>hell</u>, so forcing Shylock to <u>convert</u> to Christianity might have been seen as giving him a <u>second chance</u> at <u>salvation</u>.

2) Antonio, on the other hand, <u>isn't punished</u> for his verbal and physical abuse of Shylock. He doesn't <u>deserve</u> to lose a <u>pound of flesh</u> for his <u>prejudice</u>, but the <u>outcome</u> of the trial makes the audience wonder if he should get away with it <u>entirely</u>.

KEY QUOTE

"The quality of mercy is not strained"

Portia tells Shylock that she can't make him show mercy — he has to want to show it. That said, the way she treats Shylock at the end of Act 4, Scene 1 shows that she isn't too keen on showing mercy herself...

Love

For all the hatred to be found in *The Merchant of Venice*, there's plenty of love to balance it out.
However, even something as cheery as love creates its fair share of trouble as the play goes on.

Marriage wasn't always all about love...

1) England and Venice in the 16th century were <u>patriarchal societies</u> — men held <u>authority</u> over women. In <u>wealthy</u> families, <u>fathers</u> decided who their <u>daughters</u> should marry. This meant that <u>noblewomen</u> were usually married according to what <u>benefited</u> their families most in terms of <u>wealth</u> and <u>status</u>.

2) In Elizabethan times, men often got a <u>dowry</u> when they married — a <u>fortune</u> given to them by the <u>bride's family</u>. This makes Portia's <u>wealth</u> part of her <u>appeal</u>.

3) Bassanio knows Portia is <u>rich</u>. He's in <u>debt</u> to Antonio, which means love might not be his <u>only</u> reason for <u>marrying</u> Portia — he could do with the <u>money</u> too.

4) Marriage between <u>Christians</u> and <u>Jews</u> was <u>forbidden</u> in 16th-century Venice, so Jessica has to <u>convert</u> to Christianity to <u>marry Lorenzo</u>. This gives her another reason for marrying Lorenzo — she could <u>partly</u> be doing it to <u>escape</u> her Jewish background.

5) In the 16th century, <u>everyone</u> was expected to get married. Those who remained <u>single</u> were treated as <u>outsiders</u> later in life. This could explain why Gratiano and Nerissa <u>rush</u> into marrying each other.

... but love is important to some of the characters

1) In the play, Shakespeare suggests that <u>love</u> and <u>companionship</u> are also important in <u>marriage</u>.

2) Portia wants to <u>choose</u> her husband — she doesn't want to <u>marry</u> someone she <u>doesn't love</u>. She does end up <u>happily married</u>, but she's <u>lucky</u>. The man who picks the <u>right casket</u> happens to be the man she <u>loves</u>.

> "Beshrew me but I love her heartily"
>
> Act 2, Scene 6

3) Love is the <u>main motivation</u> for Lorenzo marrying Jessica. He knows how <u>controversial</u> it is for a <u>Christian</u> to marry a <u>converted Jew</u>, but loves Jessica <u>too much to care</u>.

Courtly love can seem a bit false

1) <u>Courtly love</u> was a way of <u>wooing</u> a lady that became popular in <u>medieval literature</u>. The man <u>idolised</u> the lady he loved, often writing poetry and songs in <u>praise</u> of her.

2) Bassanio sometimes speaks to Portia using the <u>poetic</u> and <u>exaggerated</u> language of a <u>courtly lover</u>.

3) When Bassanio's praise of Portia goes <u>over the top</u>, his love seems <u>less genuine</u>. This adds to the sense that he might be acting out of his desire for <u>wealth</u> as well as his <u>affection</u> for Portia.

> "Fair Portia's counterfeit! What demi-god Hath come so near creation?"
>
> Act 3, Scene 2

4) Courtly lovers often expressed how <u>painful</u> it was for them to be in love. Bassanio <u>dramatically</u> refers to this when he compares waiting to take the casket test to <u>torture</u> — "For as I am, <u>I live upon the rack</u>."

Love

Male friendship is a form of love...

1) The play features lots of close <u>male friendships</u>.

2) The Christian men are openly <u>affectionate</u> and tease one another. This shows how <u>close</u> and <u>comfortable</u> they are in each other's company.

3) These <u>friendships</u> make Shylock appear <u>isolated</u>. His <u>only</u> friend in the play is <u>Tubal</u>, and there's no evidence to suggest that they're <u>particularly close</u>.

4) Antonio and Bassanio's friendship <u>stands out</u> as particularly <u>deep</u>. Antonio offers Bassanio his "<u>extremest means</u>" to help him, and Bassanio offers to give up his <u>own life</u> to save Antonio's.

5) This friendship <u>drives</u> the <u>plot</u>. Without it, Antonio <u>wouldn't</u> have borrowed the money in the <u>first place</u>.

© Manuel Harlan

Character — Antonio

Some interpretations of the play portray Antonio as a <u>homosexual</u> character who is in love with Bassanio. This idea is never <u>stated</u>, but it could explain Antonio's <u>sadness</u>. He's also the only <u>unmarried</u> major character in the final scene.

... but it clashes with romantic love

1) The <u>love</u> between Antonio and Bassanio comes into <u>conflict</u> with Bassanio's love for Portia.

2) This conflict is highlighted by <u>Portia's ring</u> — when Bassanio gives it away at Antonio's request, he reveals that his <u>friendship</u> with Antonio is <u>more important</u> to him than his <u>relationship</u> with Portia.

3) Portia is <u>dissatisfied</u> with being <u>lower</u> down in Bassanio's <u>priorities</u> than Antonio, which is why she tricks him in the play's final scene — she and Nerissa want their husbands to value <u>their wives</u> over <u>their friends</u>.

Love between family members is complicated

1) Family love is another source of <u>conflict</u> in the play.

2) Portia's father has left her in a <u>difficult position</u> — she's <u>torn</u> between her <u>own</u> wishes and her <u>father's</u> desire to let the <u>caskets</u> choose a husband <u>for her</u>.

3) Portia could <u>disobey</u> her father, but she <u>obeys</u> his wishes. It isn't clear why she does this — it could be out of <u>love</u> for him, or because she sees it as her <u>duty</u> as a daughter to show him <u>respect</u>.

Shakespeare's Techniques — Language

In Act 1, Scene 2, Portia is <u>resentful</u> at being <u>held back</u> by her father's wishes — "so is the will of a <u>living</u> daughter curbed by the will of a <u>dead</u> father." The <u>antithesis</u> (see p.52) of "living" and "dead" shows how <u>frustrating</u> she finds it to be <u>controlled</u> by someone who isn't even <u>alive</u>.

4) Jessica shows <u>little love</u> or <u>respect</u> for her father. She knows that it will <u>hurt</u> Shylock to lose his <u>daughter</u> and a lot of his <u>money</u>, but goes ahead with her escape plan <u>anyway</u>.

5) In the 16th century, daughters were expected to <u>obey</u> their fathers. This made it <u>shameful</u> for a daughter to <u>abandon</u> her father as Jessica does. However, the <u>unflattering</u> portrayal of Shylock as a father means that Shakespeare's audience might have seen Jessica's betrayal as <u>acceptable</u>.

KEY QUOTE

"Come, away! / For you shall hence upon your wedding-day"

Portia lets Bassanio sail away on their wedding day, but she refuses to let him prioritise his friendship over his marriage much longer. Her trick is intended to remind Bassanio that he should always put his wife first.

Appearance and Reality

You've probably been told not to judge a book by its cover, but it's safe to assume no one's ever warned you not to judge a casket by its appearance. If only someone had warned the Princes of Morocco and Aragon...

Appearances mean a lot to the characters...

1) <u>Outward appearances</u> are important to many of the play's characters, but for <u>different reasons</u>.

2) Some characters believe that appearances are <u>crucial</u> to making a <u>good impression</u> on others.

3) The Prince of Morocco boasts about his <u>good looks</u>, saying that "<u>The best-regarded virgins</u>" in Morocco love him because he's so <u>handsome</u>. He wrongly assumes that this will <u>impress</u> Portia.

> **Character — Portia**
>
> Portia claims that she isn't "<u>solely led</u>" by the <u>appearance</u> of her suitors, but even she judges them according to what they <u>look like</u> at times. In Act 1, Scene 2, she mocks an Englishman for his dress sense — "<u>How oddly he is suited</u>!"

4) Other characters associate outward appearances with <u>maintaining</u> their <u>influence</u> and <u>reputation</u>.

5) Bassanio describes Portia's other suitors as "<u>Renownèd</u>" and tells Antonio he can't "<u>hold a rival place</u>" with them without <u>Antonio's help</u>. He needs to appear <u>wealthy</u> to be viewed as a <u>potential husband</u>.

6) The Duke is <u>preoccupied</u> with how Venice appears to <u>foreign traders</u> — it's <u>important</u> to him that they see it as a place where they'll be treated <u>fairly</u>.

7) The Duke's decision not to <u>break the law</u> to save Antonio's life reveals his <u>anxiety</u> at maintaining the city's <u>reputation</u>.

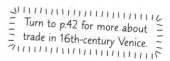

Turn to p.42 for more about trade in 16th-century Venice.

... but appearances can be deceptive

© Donald Cooper/photostage

1) In the play, Shakespeare <u>warns against</u> attaching too much <u>significance</u> to <u>appearances</u>. His message to the audience is that not everything is always <u>as it seems</u>.

2) The <u>ending</u> shows that the law in Venice isn't as <u>fair</u> as the Duke thinks. Shylock is <u>punished</u>, but Antonio suffers <u>no consequences</u> for treating Shylock unfairly.

3) <u>Mercy</u> is seen <u>differently</u> by <u>different characters</u> (see p.37). Antonio and the other Christians think they're being <u>merciful</u> to Shylock at the end of the trial, but it's unlikely that Shylock thinks the <u>same</u> — their <u>punishments</u> are <u>devastating</u> for him.

4) Shylock thinks he has a daughter that he can <u>control</u>, but the <u>obedient</u> impression Jessica gives him in Act 2, Scene 5 is <u>misleading</u>. It's only when Jessica <u>runs away</u> with Lorenzo and <u>steals</u> from Shylock that he realises her <u>true nature</u>.

5) Similarly, when Portia gets engaged to Bassanio, she gives the impression she'll <u>submit</u> to him — she calls him her "<u>lord</u>", "<u>governor</u>" and "<u>king</u>". In spite of this, she uses her ring to <u>gain authority</u> in their relationship.

> **Characters — Jessica and Portia**
>
> Seeing a <u>different side</u> to a character can change the audience's <u>perception</u> of them. Jessica seems <u>selfish</u> for <u>stealing</u> from Shylock and <u>spending</u> the money recklessly, but Portia's <u>trickery</u> makes her more <u>likeable</u> by showing that she's <u>brave</u> and <u>spirited</u>.

Appearance and Reality

There's more to the caskets than meets the eye

1) The poems found in each casket tell the audience that judging something by its appearance is unwise:

Gold Casket

"All that glitters is not gold;
Often have you heard that told" — the gold casket suggests that the appearance of something doesn't necessarily indicate its true value.

Silver Casket

"Some there be that shadows kiss;
Such have but a shadow's bliss" — the silver casket says that those who obsess over their own reflection will never experience true happiness.

Lead Casket

"You that choose not by the view,
Chance as fair and choose as true" — the lead casket demonstrates that judging something by more than its outward appearance is wise.

2) The Prince of Morocco picks the gold casket because it's the only one as beautiful as Portia. His superficial reasoning leads to failure — he's made to look like a fool for being shallow.

3) The Prince of Aragon recognises that it's foolish to "choose by show", but dismisses the lead casket as "base" (common). He's too proud to consider that such a casket might contain what he deserves.

4) Bassanio is drawn to the lead casket because its humble appearance promises him nothing. He knows that looks can be deceiving, and is rewarded for picking the least attractive casket.

Disguises entertain the audience...

1) Disguises are a key feature of the plot — Portia and Nerissa use them to save Antonio, and Jessica uses one to escape from Shylock's house.

2) In Elizabethan theatre, the actors were always male. This would have made the masculine disguises in the play particularly funny, because the female characters were already being played by men.

3) Portia and Nerissa's disguises create dramatic irony. The fact that Bassanio and Gratiano can't recognise their wives entertains the audience — they find it funny to watch the men get into trouble.

Context — Women in Venice

In 16th-century Venice, women had a limited role in public life. Wearing male clothing allows Portia to rebel against these restrictions — her disguise is what lets her intervene in Antonio's trial, as women weren't allowed to be lawyers.

© Moviestore Collection/REX/Shutterstock

... and are used to highlight the characters' flaws

1) Portia uses her disguise to test Bassanio's loyalty. In Act 3, Scene 2, he swears to keep his ring, saying that "when this ring / Parts from this finger, then parts life from hence". In reality, however, he's easily persuaded to give it up by Antonio.

2) Nerissa uses her disguise in the same way — when Gratiano gives up his ring, the audience sees that he's not as dedicated to Nerissa as the "oaths of love" he swore to her before would suggest.

Think about the wider significance of the casket test...

The casket test isn't just a means of finding a husband — it also lets the audience know appearances aren't all they're cracked up to be. Think about how this message applies to other parts of the play.

Wealth

Money is at the heart of just about everything in the play — it's a theme you can't afford to forget...

Venice was a rich and powerful state

1) 16th-century Venice was at the centre of Mediterranean trade routes. The constant flow of goods in and out of the city made it very prosperous.

2) Jews were important to the economy. Unlike Christians, they were allowed to practise usury (charging interest on loans), and their profits were heavily taxed by the state.

3) This explains why the Duke can't treat Shylock unfairly in Act 4, Scene 1 — he can't risk upsetting the Jewish community, as they are a valuable source of income.

© ERREBI/REX/Shutterstock

4) Setting the play in a city that revolves around money and trade allows Shakespeare to explore ideas of value and worth. He questions whether any of the characters are able to set aside their desire for wealth.

Money is central to the plot...

Head to p.47 for more on plots and sub-plots.

1) The main plot of *The Merchant of Venice* hinges on Shylock's loan and Antonio's failure to repay it. Money is part of the reason they hate each other in the first place — Antonio is opposed to lending money for profit, but Shylock's entire livelihood is based on doing exactly that.

2) Money is also an important feature in some of the play's sub-plots:

- Portia's vast wealth prompts suitors to come to Belmont from "the four corners of the earth". Her father created the casket test to find Portia a husband who values her for more than just her money.

- When Jessica runs away from Shylock, she steals a lot of his money and spends it recklessly. Shakespeare uses Shylock's reaction to explore if he values money more than his daughter.

... and at the forefront of the characters' minds

1) Shakespeare suggests that Bassanio wants to marry Portia to clear his debts. The first thing he tells Antonio about her is that she's "richly left" — her other qualities aren't as important.

> ### Shakespeare's Techniques — Language
>
> The close link between love and money in the characters' minds is reflected in the language they use to talk about marriage. When Bassanio passes the test of the caskets, he refuses to believe his engagement to Portia until it's "signed" and "ratified" by her. This takes away from the romance by making it sound like a business transaction.

2) Shylock is also attached to his money. He finds the cost of Jessica's betrayal more upsetting than actually losing his daughter — "The thief gone with so much, and so much to find the thief."

3) Antonio is an exception to the play's money-driven characters. He starts and finishes the play rich, but his melancholy state proves that money alone doesn't make him happy. His willingness to take on a large debt so that Bassanio can woo Portia suggests that he values love over money.

KEY QUOTE

"Three thousand ducats; 'tis a good round sum."

Three thousand ducats is more than "a good round sum" — it's an absolute fortune. There's a huge amount of money at stake in *The Merchant of Venice*, so it's no surprise the characters can't stop thinking about it.

Prejudice

Prejudice is no laughing matter, but this particular comedy is full of it. Read on to find out more...

Religious prejudice was common

Prejudice towards Jews is called anti-Semitism.

1) In 16th-century Venice, Jews had little <u>freedom</u> — they were <u>denied</u> the right to become Venetian <u>citizens</u> or <u>own land</u>, and were forced to live together in a <u>separate</u> part of the city called a <u>ghetto</u>. Antonio's <u>abuse</u> of Shylock in public reflects the open <u>anti-Semitism</u> experienced by Jews at the time.

2) Shylock has a <u>hostile</u> attitude to the Christian characters — he refuses to "<u>eat</u>", "<u>drink</u>" or "<u>pray</u>" with them. This shows the <u>religious</u> and <u>cultural divide</u> between Jews and Christians in the 16th century.

3) Jews were <u>expelled</u> from England in 1290 and weren't <u>allowed</u> to <u>return</u> until the mid-17th century. This means that Shakespeare's audiences had <u>limited contact</u> with Jews. Their opinion of them was based on what they were <u>told</u>, so they probably <u>wouldn't</u> have questioned the play's <u>negative portrayal</u> of Shylock.

Hatred is deep-rooted in the play

1) In Act 1, Scene 3, Shylock tells the audience that he <u>hates</u> Antonio "for he is a <u>Christian</u>". His <u>loathing</u> of Antonio drives his desire for <u>revenge</u> in the play.

2) There's no end in sight to their <u>hostility</u>. Both characters keep acting on their <u>hatred</u> despite the <u>problems</u> it causes.

3) For example, Antonio tells Shylock he would "<u>spit on thee again</u>", and Shylock admits that he has "<u>no firm reason</u>" for taking Antonio's flesh other than to <u>satisfy</u> his "<u>hate</u>" for him.

4) <u>Hatred</u> doesn't only exist between Antonio and Shylock — all of the Christian characters are <u>anti-Semitic</u> to some extent. This shows that <u>prejudice</u> was part of the <u>society</u> they lived in.

Shakespeare's Techniques — Imagery

Hostility towards Shylock <u>peaks</u> during the <u>court scene</u>. This is reflected in the <u>imagery</u> used by the <u>Christians</u> to describe Shylock. The <u>Duke</u> calls him an "<u>inhuman wretch</u>", while <u>Gratiano</u> describes his desire for a pound of flesh as "<u>wolvish</u>". This makes Shylock seem <u>monstrous</u>.

Attitudes change over time

1) The <u>prejudice</u> shown towards Shylock and others in the play is a <u>good example</u> of how something that was <u>normal</u> (or even <u>funny</u>) to a 16th-century audience can be <u>shocking</u> to a <u>modern audience</u>.

© United Archives GmbH / Alamy Stock Photo

2) A <u>modern audience</u> might <u>sympathise</u> more with Shylock. A 16th-century audience would have <u>shared</u> the Christian characters' <u>prejudices</u>, but a modern audience is more likely to think that Shylock is <u>unfairly persecuted</u>.

3) The way Portia <u>mocks</u> her suitors using <u>national stereotypes</u> in Act 1, Scene 2 is meant to be <u>funny</u>, but it might be seen as <u>offensive</u> by modern audiences. Her casual <u>racism</u> about the Prince of Morocco's "<u>complexion</u>" is also <u>unacceptable</u> from a <u>modern perspective</u>.

EXAM TIP

Consider how different audiences might react to the play...

No two audiences are the same, especially when they're separated by over four hundred years. You need to prove that you understand the differences in attitude between modern and Shakespearean audiences.

Practice Questions

Themes, themes, good for your heart, the more you know, the more you... get marks. Themes are vital to your understanding of the play, but they're no good on their own — you also need to show that you're aware of the context surrounding them. These questions should help you get to grips with the ideas covered in this section.

Quick Questions

1) Why does Shylock think the courtroom is the only place he'll get justice?

2) In what way are the Christian characters hypocrites?

3) What is a 'patriarchal society'?

4) Why must Jessica convert to Christianity before marrying Lorenzo?

5) Give one example of how Bassanio behaves like a courtly lover.

6) Which two words best describe the nature of appearances in the play?
   a) dependable   b) reliable   c) false   d) misleading   e) trustworthy

7) In the 16th century, what made it so funny to see female characters dressed as men?

8) What business could Jews practise that Christians couldn't in 16th-century Venice?

9) Explain what is meant by the term 'anti-Semitism'.

10) Why did people have limited contact with Jews in Elizabethan England?

In-depth Questions

1) What is the difference between the views on punishment expressed in the Old Testament and New Testament? How is this difference reflected in the play?

2) Choose two types of love that feature in the play and explain how they come into conflict with each other. Support your answer using quotes and examples from the play.

3) How does Shakespeare use the caskets to show that appearances can be deceptive?

4) Explain why the Duke can't bend the rules in Antonio's favour in Act 4, Scene 1. Refer to the context surrounding the play to support your answer.

5) Who is most to blame for the play's main feud: Antonio or Shylock? Explain your answer.

Practice Questions

You're bound to write about themes in the exam, so it's a good idea to get some practice in. Tackle these questions now and you'll be well on your way to writing top quality essays when the pressure's really on.

Exam-style Questions

1) Read the extract below, then answer the questions.

> | **Bassanio:** | For thy three thousand ducats here is six. |
> | **Shylock:** | If every ducat in six thousand ducats |
> | | Were in six parts and every part a ducat, |
> | | I would not draw them; I would have my bond. |
> | **Duke:** | How shalt thou hope for mercy, rendering none? |
> | **Shylock:** | What judgment shall I dread, doing no wrong? |
> | | You have among you many a purchased slave, |
> | | Which, like your asses and your dogs and mules, |
> | | You use in abject and in slavish parts, |
> | | Because you bought them: shall I say to you, |
> | | Let them be free, marry them to your heirs? |
> | | Why sweat they under burdens? Let their beds |
> | | Be made as soft as yours and let their palates |
> | | Be seasoned with such viands? You will answer |
> | | 'The slaves are ours.' So do I answer you: |
> | | The pound of flesh, which I demand of him, |
> | | Is dearly bought; 'tis mine and I will have it. |
> | | If you deny me, fie upon your law! |
> | | There is no force in the decrees of Venice. |
> | | I stand for judgment: answer; shall I have it? |
>
> (Act 4, Scene 1)

   a) How does Shakespeare present the character of Shylock in this extract?

   b) In this extract, Shylock refuses to show mercy to Antonio. Explain the importance of mercy elsewhere in the play. You should consider:

- different ideas about mercy
- the role of mercy in the play.

2) Read Act 2, Scene 5 from "**I am bid forth to supper, Jessica**" to "**Say I will come.**" How is prejudice presented in this extract and elsewhere in the play?

3) Read Act 3, Scene 2 from "**So may the outward shows**" to "**joy be the consequence!**" Explain the importance of false appearances in this extract and in the rest of the play.

4) Read Act 2, Scene 6 from "**Who are you?**" to "**Shall she be placèd in my constant soul.**" How does Shakespeare present romantic love in this extract and elsewhere in the play?

Form and Structure of 'The Merchant of Venice'

If *The Merchant of Venice* was a ship, then form and structure would be the nails holding all of the planks together — they're pretty important to the play. Without them, it would be an absolute wreck...

'The Merchant of Venice' is a comedy...

1) Shakespeare's plays are usually <u>comedies</u>, <u>tragedies</u> or <u>histories</u>. *The Merchant of Venice* includes lots of features of a <u>comedy</u>:

- Puns and wordplay
- Comic misunderstandings
- Disguises
- Marriage
- A clown character
- A happy ending

© Donald Cooper/photostage

2) Another <u>common feature</u> of Shakespeare's comedies is a couple who have to <u>overcome</u> a problem to be together. <u>Bassanio and Portia</u> and <u>Lorenzo and Jessica</u> are good examples of this.

Theme — Love

In Shakespeare's comedies, a <u>common problem</u> faced by lovers is their <u>parents' wishes</u>. Portia's father <u>stops</u> her from marrying who she <u>wants</u>, and Shylock's hatred of Christians means Jessica has to <u>elope</u> to be with Lorenzo.

... but it also has elements of a tragedy

1) The main plot of *The Merchant of Venice* addresses <u>serious</u> themes like <u>prejudice</u> and <u>justice</u>. This is <u>unusual</u> for a comedy, because the <u>main focus</u> is usually on <u>love</u>. This creates <u>uncertainty</u> — comedies normally end <u>happily</u>, but the <u>dark subject matter</u> makes the audience doubt whether this one will too.

2) Not all of the characters have a <u>happy ending</u>. Shylock loses almost <u>everything</u> and Antonio is <u>isolated</u> — he loses his <u>best friend</u> to Portia and is the only main character left <u>unmarried</u>.

3) Shakespeare also questions whether <u>everyone</u> will stay happy for long. For example, in Act 2, Gratiano implies that love is "<u>with more spirit chasèd than enjoyed</u>". This hints that his love for Nerissa will <u>fade</u> as time passes.

4) Shylock can be viewed as a <u>tragic character</u>. His <u>suffering</u> seems <u>unfair</u>, as he's a victim of <u>prejudice</u> from Christians.

Theme — Prejudice

<u>Anti-Semitism</u> was much more <u>common</u> in the 16th century, so Shakespeare's audiences are <u>unlikely</u> to have seen Shylock's <u>suffering</u> as <u>tragic</u>. Most 16th-century productions would have presented him as a <u>villain</u>.

The play has a five act structure

Acts 1, 2 and 3 lead to the <u>climax</u> in Act 4, and most of the <u>loose ends</u> are tied up in Act 5:

- Act 1 introduces the <u>main characters</u> and the <u>feud</u> between Antonio and Shylock.
- Act 2 develops some of the <u>sub-plots</u>. Jessica <u>runs away</u> and Portia meets two more suitors.
- Act 3 introduces a problem in the <u>main plot</u>. Antonio <u>can't repay</u> Shylock, so his life is at risk.
- Act 4 sees the action reach a <u>climax</u>. Portia <u>saves</u> Antonio after a <u>tense</u> confrontation in court.
- Act 5 is the <u>resolution</u>. Everyone learns <u>the truth</u> and the couples are <u>happily reconciled</u>.

Form and Structure of 'The Merchant of Venice'

Shakespeare swaps between storylines...

1) The main plot follows the agreement between Antonio and Shylock and its consequences.

2) The sub-plots help Shakespeare to control the mood of the play and develop different themes:

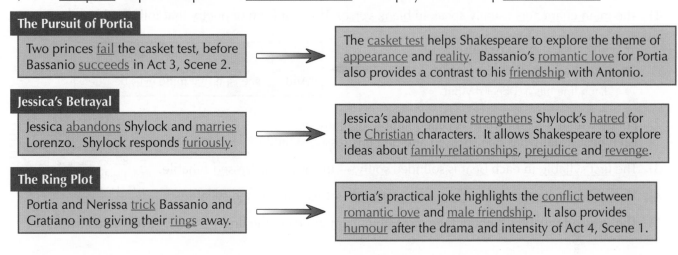

The Pursuit of Portia

Two princes fail the casket test, before Bassanio succeeds in Act 3, Scene 2.

→ The casket test helps Shakespeare to explore the theme of appearance and reality. Bassanio's romantic love for Portia also provides a contrast to his friendship with Antonio.

Jessica's Betrayal

Jessica abandons Shylock and marries Lorenzo. Shylock responds furiously.

→ Jessica's abandonment strengthens Shylock's hatred for the Christian characters. It allows Shakespeare to explore ideas about family relationships, prejudice and revenge.

The Ring Plot

Portia and Nerissa trick Bassanio and Gratiano into giving their rings away.

→ Portia's practical joke highlights the conflict between romantic love and male friendship. It also provides humour after the drama and intensity of Act 4, Scene 1.

... and uses structure to control tension

1) Swapping between different plots creates suspense — important issues are left unresolved, which makes the audience wonder what will happen. For example, the Prince of Morocco arrives at Belmont in Act 2, Scene 1, but he doesn't take the casket test until Act 2, Scene 7.

2) Long scenes create tension too. Act 4, Scene 1 is the play's longest scene — the audience watches the whole trial without any interruptions, which means that the drama builds as the scene goes on.

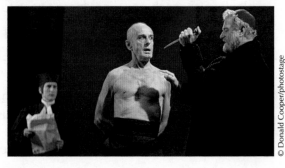

© Donald Cooper/photostage

3) Comic scenes help the tension rise and fall. Lancelet's clownish behaviour in Act 3, Scene 5 comes directly before the tense court scene. The humour in this scene relieves the tension so it can be built up again in Act 4.

Shakespeare gives clues about what might happen

1) The play sometimes hints at what might happen later — this is known as foreshadowing. Foreshadowing plants an idea in the audience's mind without guaranteeing that it will happen. This creates anticipation.

2) In Act 1, Salerio mentions the danger of running aground in the "shallows" and Shylock talks about the "peril of waters". Their comments foreshadow the news in Act 3, Scene 2 that Antonio has lost his ships.

3) After Shylock agrees to lend him money, Antonio says "The Hebrew will turn Christian: he grows kind." This comment foreshadows the way that Shylock is forced to convert to Christianity in Act 4, Scene 1.

Explain how Shakespeare holds the audience's attention...

Whether it's joke after joke or non-stop drama, too much of the same thing gets boring very quickly. Shakespeare mixes it up by weaving several different storylines together — both comic and tragic.

Poetry and Prose

Roses are red, Portia is picky, poetry's tough and prose is quite tricky. Luckily for you, these pages will tell you all you need to know about poetry and prose — it's technical in places, but nothing you can't handle.

'The Merchant of Venice' is mostly written in blank verse...

1) The <u>main characters</u> usually speak in <u>blank verse</u>. This is a form of <u>poetry</u> that follows these <u>three rules</u>:

   - The lines usually <u>don't rhyme</u>.
   - Each line has <u>10</u> or <u>11</u> syllables.
   - Each line has a <u>5-beat</u> rhythm.

1	2	3	4	5

   "And <u>fair</u> she <u>is</u>, if <u>that</u> mine <u>eyes</u> be <u>true</u>"

2) Poetry with a 5-beat rhythm is called <u>iambic pentameter</u>. Each beat usually has one <u>stressed</u> and one <u>unstressed</u> syllable.

   Iambic pentameter can be rhymed or unrhymed. Blank verse never has a regular rhyme pattern.

3) The <u>first syllable</u> in each <u>beat</u> is sounded <u>softly</u> — this is an <u>unstressed</u> syllable.

4) The <u>second syllable</u> in each <u>beat</u> is <u>emphasised</u> — this is a <u>stressed</u> syllable.

5) The <u>stressed</u> syllables <u>highlight</u> the most <u>significant</u> words in the line — "fair", "eyes" and "true".

... but there's plenty of prose too

1) <u>Prose</u> has no set <u>rhyme</u> or <u>rhythm</u> — it sounds like <u>everyday</u> speech.

2) If a passage is written in <u>prose</u>, it will look like a <u>paragraph</u>. Unlike blank verse, each <u>new line</u> doesn't have to start with a <u>capital letter</u>.

3) In Shakespeare's plays, prose is often used in scenes about <u>everyday life</u> or for <u>rude comedy</u>. This means that it's usually associated with characters with a <u>lower status</u> — Lancelet and <u>his father</u> speak in prose.

4) As prose doesn't have to follow a certain <u>pattern</u>, it can be much more <u>straightforward</u> than verse. This makes it useful for <u>narrating</u> important <u>plot details</u> to the audience. For example, Antonio's <u>letter</u> to Bassanio detailing the <u>loss of his ships</u> is written in prose in Act 3, Scene 2.

© Jane Hobson/REX/Shutterstock

Rhymed verse appears less often

1) Each of the caskets contains a <u>rhymed poem</u>. These poems <u>stand out</u>, as most of the play is <u>unrhymed</u>. This helps Shakespeare to highlight the <u>moral message</u> in each of the poems to the <u>audience</u>.

   "You that choose not by the **view**,
   Chance as fair and choose as **true**!
   Since this fortune falls to **you**,
   Be content and seek no **new**."
   Act 3, Scene 2

2) After Bassanio chooses the right casket, he makes a speech in <u>rhymed verse</u>. This echoes the poetic language of <u>courtly lovers</u> (see p.38), which gives his speech a <u>romantic tone</u>.

3) Rhyme can provide a <u>decisive</u> end to a scene. Gratiano marks the end of Act 2, Scene 6 with a <u>rhyming couplet</u>. This emphasises that he's about to <u>set sail</u> with Bassanio.

   "I am glad on't: I desire no more **delight**
   Than to be under sail and gone **tonight**."
   Act 2, Scene 6

Poetry and Prose

Blank verse has different effects

1) The <u>regular rhythm</u> of <u>blank verse</u> can create <u>fast-paced</u> dialogue between the characters.

> Bassanio: Do all men kill the things they do not love?
> Shylock: Hates any man the thing he would not kill?
> Bassanio: Every offence is not a hate at first.
> *Act 4, Scene 1*

2) In Act 4, Scene 1, Shakespeare uses lots of these <u>quick exchanges</u> to add to the <u>tense atmosphere</u> between <u>hostile characters</u> in the courtroom.

3) At the start of Act 5, Scene 1, Lorenzo and Jessica declare their <u>love</u> for one another in <u>blank verse</u>. The way that they <u>complete</u> each other's lines of <u>iambic pentameter</u> highlights how <u>close</u> they are.

4) When Bassanio uses <u>blank verse</u> with lots of <u>extravagant imagery</u>, it can seem a bit <u>artificial</u>. This is because it makes his speech sound less <u>natural</u>.

5) In Act 3, Scene 2, it causes his <u>reaction</u> to the <u>engagement</u> to sound very <u>formal</u> — this makes his <u>love</u> for Portia seem a bit <u>forced</u>.

> "Madam, you have bereft me of all words,
> Only my blood speaks to you in my veins"
> *Act 3, Scene 2*

Character — Bassanio

The fact that Bassanio's <u>speech</u> with Portia sounds <u>forced</u> at times doesn't necessarily mean he has <u>no feelings</u> for her. Shakespeare wants the <u>audience</u> to <u>question</u> if love is his <u>only</u> reason for marrying her.

Some characters use blank verse and prose

1) Some characters <u>switch</u> between <u>blank verse</u> and <u>prose</u>, depending on <u>who</u> they're talking to and <u>how</u> they feel.

2) Although Portia and Nerissa <u>generally</u> speak to others in <u>verse</u>, they speak to one another in <u>prose</u> for the whole of Act 1, Scene 2. This more <u>informal</u> way of speaking suggests they feel <u>comfortable</u> when they're <u>together</u>.

© Donald Cooper/photostage

3) In Act 3, Scene 1, Shylock uses prose to discuss Jessica's <u>betrayal</u>. This allows Shakespeare to emphasise Shylock's <u>shock</u> and <u>distress</u>, as the <u>irregular rhythm</u> of his speech highlights his <u>lack of composure</u>.

> "No news of them? Why, so: and I know not what's spent in the search: why, thou loss upon loss!"
> *Act 3, Scene 1*

Character — Shylock

Shylock uses prose more <u>regularly</u> than any other <u>major character</u>. This is a way for Shakespeare to further emphasise Shylock's status as an <u>outsider</u>.

4) In Act 4, Scene 1, Shylock <u>switches</u> to speaking in <u>prose</u> when Portia asks him if he has scales to weigh Antonio's flesh. His abrupt response ("<u>I have them ready</u>.") disrupts the <u>rhythm</u> of the dialogue, which makes his <u>cold ambition</u> to kill Antonio <u>stand out</u>. This adds to the <u>menacing atmosphere</u> of the scene.

EXAM TIP

Consider why the characters speak the way they do...

There isn't a clear rule for when characters use prose or blank verse, but it's important that you learn to recognise which is which. Once you can do that, it'll be easier to write about their effects in the exam.

Imagery and Symbolism

Shakespeare liked to spice up his plays with a range of imagery — *The Merchant of Venice* is no exception.

Religious imagery emphasises religious conflict

1) Shakespeare uses <u>religious imagery</u> to highlight the <u>conflict</u> between the <u>Christian</u> and <u>Jewish</u> characters.

2) The Christians often refer to Shylock as the "<u>devil</u>". This <u>metaphor</u> shows how <u>villainous</u> Shylock is in their eyes, as the devil is associated with <u>evil</u>. It also reflects their <u>belief</u> that Jews were destined to go to <u>hell</u>.

3) Religious imagery is used a lot in the <u>court scene</u>:

> • When Shylock believes Portia will rule in his favour, he calls her "a <u>Daniel</u>" to praise her <u>wise judgment</u>.
>
> • Gratiano <u>mocks</u> Shylock later in the scene by <u>repeating</u> the <u>same imagery</u> — "A <u>second Daniel</u>, a Daniel, Jew!"
>
> • Portia uses a <u>simile</u> to stress the <u>divine nature</u> of mercy to Shylock — "It droppeth <u>as the gentle rain from heaven</u>".

Daniel is...

... a <u>wise</u> Jewish figure in the <u>Old Testament</u>. He intervenes in the trial of a woman called Susanna and <u>saves her life</u> by proving that she's <u>innocent</u>. This explains why Shylock calls Portia "a <u>Daniel</u>" — he thinks she's going to give him the <u>justice</u> he <u>deserves</u>.

Mythological imagery is used to describe love

1) Several characters refer to Greek and Roman <u>mythology</u> when they're talking about <u>love</u>.

2) Bassanio uses a <u>metaphor</u> to describe Portia's <u>suitors</u>. He says they are "<u>Jasons</u> come in <u>quest</u> of her", which makes pursuing Portia seem <u>heroic</u> and presents her as a <u>prize</u> worth taking <u>risks</u> for. This image is intended to <u>persuade</u> Antonio to help him.

3) Portia compares Bassanio's attempt at the <u>casket test</u> to the rescue of Hesione by <u>Hercules</u> (also known as "<u>Alcides</u>"). This shows how <u>tense</u> this moment is by suggesting that her <u>life depends</u> on Bassanio choosing the <u>correct casket</u>.

Jason and Hercules are...

... heroes from <u>Greek mythology</u>. Jason had to overcome a series of <u>dangerous obstacles</u> to find the <u>Golden Fleece</u>, while Hercules is known for <u>brave deeds</u> such as saving <u>Hesione</u> (a princess) from a sea monster.

4) Lorenzo and Jessica use <u>mythological imagery</u> to describe their relationship in Act 5, Scene 1. They compare themselves to <u>doomed lovers</u> (see p.22), which suggests their relationship may <u>not</u> end well.

Commercial imagery is used in different ways

1) In Act 1, Scene 1, Salerio describes a <u>shipwreck</u> using <u>personification</u>. The image of the ship bending over "<u>her ribs</u>" to "<u>kiss her burial</u>" makes it seem like a <u>living being</u>, which highlights that it's <u>important</u> to him.

2) Bassanio uses imagery relating to <u>commerce</u> to describe his <u>engagement</u> to Portia. In Act 3, Scene 2, he makes their marriage sound like a <u>business deal</u>.

> "As doubtful whether what I see be true,
> Until **confirmed**, **signed**, **ratified** by you."
>
> Act 3, Scene 2

© Nigel Norrington / ArenaPAL

3) In the same scene, Portia says the test of the caskets puts "<u>bars</u> between the <u>owners</u> and their <u>rights</u>". This image shows that Portia views marriage in terms of <u>ownership</u> too — even in her mind, a wife <u>belongs</u> to her husband.

Imagery and Symbolism

The caskets symbolise Christian values

1) The casket test teaches the suitors important <u>Christian values</u>:

- The <u>gold casket</u> warns against basing decisions on <u>desire</u>. The Prince of Morocco does this when he chooses gold for its <u>value</u>.
- The <u>silver casket</u> stresses the importance of <u>modesty</u>. The Prince of Aragon chooses silver <u>unwisely</u> because he's so <u>arrogant</u>.
- The <u>lead casket</u> represents <u>faith</u>. Only Bassanio is willing to take a leap of faith and "<u>hazard all he hath</u>" in order to marry Portia.

2) The casket test also shows how Portia's father <u>influences</u> her life after his <u>death</u>. It can either be seen as a symbol of his <u>undying love</u> for Portia, or as a symbol of his <u>continued control</u> over her.

© Donald Cooper/photostage

The rings symbolise ideas about loyalty

1) The <u>rings</u> that Bassanio and Gratiano are <u>given</u> by their wives represent <u>commitment</u> and <u>faithfulness</u>.

2) When Bassanio and Gratiano <u>give away</u> their rings, Portia and Nerissa take it as a sign that they <u>don't appreciate</u> their <u>significance</u>. The trick is meant to <u>remind</u> their husbands of what the rings <u>represent</u>.

3) When Jessica abandons Shylock, she <u>steals</u> a ring given to him by his <u>wife</u>. His claim that he wouldn't have sold it "for a <u>wilderness of monkeys</u>" suggests that the ring is <u>priceless</u> to him — its main value to him is <u>sentimental</u>.

4) Shylock's ring becomes a symbol of Jessica's <u>disloyalty</u>. By <u>stealing</u> it and <u>selling</u> it, she <u>betrays</u> her father's <u>trust</u> and <u>distances herself</u> further from her <u>family</u>.

> "If you had known the virtue of the ring,
> Or half her worthiness that gave the ring,
> Or your own honour to contain the ring,
> You would not then have parted with the ring."
>
> Act 5, Scene 1

The pound of flesh represents revenge and sacrifice

1) The <u>pound of flesh</u> symbolises Shylock's <u>desire</u> for <u>revenge</u> against Antonio.

2) Antonio's flesh has no <u>practical use</u> or <u>value</u> to Shylock — he wants it because it represents <u>justice</u>.

> "if it will feed nothing else,
> it will feed my revenge."
>
> Act 3, Scene 1

Theme — Justice and Mercy

To Shylock, taking a pound of Antonio's <u>flesh</u> is <u>fair</u> — he's <u>legally entitled</u> to receive the <u>forfeit</u> set out in the <u>bond</u>. The Christian characters <u>disagree</u> — they think it's <u>wrong</u> that Shylock is using the <u>law</u> to pursue <u>revenge</u>.

3) The <u>pound of flesh</u> is also a symbol of the <u>sacrifices</u> friends make for each other. The fact that Antonio is <u>willing</u> to risk a pound of his flesh just to help Bassanio shows how much he <u>values their friendship</u>.

EXAM TIP

Learn about the different types of imagery...

Metaphor, simile, personification... these are all types of imagery. You'll really impress the examiner if you're able to identify these techniques in an extract — there's a handy table on p.61 to help you.

Other Language Techniques

Not all of Shakespeare's techniques get a page of their own — here are a few more to get your head around.

Puns create humour and reveal characters' feelings

1) A pun is a type of wordplay that plays on the different meanings of a word, or on the meanings of two words that sound the same.

2) Many puns in the play create humour. In Act 3, Scene 5, Lancelet plays on two meanings of the word "cover" — when Lorenzo asks him to "cover" ('set the table'), he purposely misinterprets the instruction as 'wear a hat'.

© Sheila Burnett / ArenaPAL

3) Not all puns have a comic effect. When Portia says "so is the will of a living daughter curbed by the will of a dead father", she uses two meanings of "will" ('wishes' and 'last will and testament'). The effect isn't humorous though — it draws attention to her frustration.

Antithesis puts two contrasting ideas together

1) Antithesis creates a contrast by putting two opposite ideas together.

2) Shakespeare uses lots of antithesis in Act 3, Scene 1 to create a tense atmosphere. He contrasts hot and cold to express Shylock's anger at Antonio for mistreating him.

> "**cooled** my friends, **heated** mine enemies"
> Act 3, Scene 1

3) In Act 5, Scene 1, Portia's contrast of "light" (unfaithful) and "heavy" (unhappy) hints at the conflict that develops between her and Bassanio later in the scene.

> "a **light** wife doth make a **heavy** husband"
> Act 5, Scene 1

Hyperbole exaggerates for effect

1) Hyperbole is exaggeration — it isn't meant to be taken literally by the other characters or the audience.

> "**all the world** desires her;"
> Act 2, Scene 7

2) Characters often use hyperbole to emphasise something. Not everyone in the world actually wants to marry Portia — it's a way for the Prince of Morocco to stress how desirable she is.

Repetition emphasises a point

1) Repetition is also used for emphasis. Shylock repeats this phrase about his bond, which stresses his preoccupation with revenge.

> "**I'll have my bond**; I will not hear thee speak:
> **I'll have my bond**; and therefore speak no more."
> Act 3, Scene 3

2) In Act 1, Scene 2, Portia repeats the word "choose" when she talks about the casket test. This shows that her inability to choose a husband is constantly on her mind and reflects how trapped she feels.

KEY QUOTE — **"We all expect a gentle answer, Jew."**

Not all puns in the play are meant to be funny. The Duke's pun on the word 'Gentile' (meaning 'not Jewish') implies that mercy is a Christian value that Jews don't understand — not exactly side-splitting...

Mood and Atmosphere

Changes in mood and atmosphere make *The Merchant of Venice* a real emotional rollercoaster — buckle up...

Different settings create different moods

1) The setting <u>switches</u> between <u>Venice</u> and <u>Belmont</u> throughout the play.

2) Most of the scenes set in <u>Venice</u> take place in the <u>street</u>. This gives the audience the impression that the characters are constantly <u>on the move</u>, which creates the atmosphere of a <u>bustling city</u>.

3) This contrasts with the <u>domestic</u> setting of <u>Belmont</u>. The <u>difference</u> between these settings is most <u>obvious</u> at the <u>end</u> of the play — the <u>dramatic</u> court scene in Venice makes Belmont seem <u>peaceful</u> in comparison.

4) Not every scene in Venice is <u>serious</u> and not every scene in Belmont is <u>happy</u> — <u>both</u> these settings have <u>tense</u> and <u>light-hearted</u> moments. For example, Portia is <u>concerned</u> about finding a husband in Act 1, Scene 2, and the Venetian characters share several <u>jokes</u> in Act 1, Scene 1.

> **Context — Gender**
>
> In 16th-century Venice, women had <u>very little influence</u> in <u>public life</u>. This is reflected in the play's two main settings — the streets of Venice are <u>dominated</u> by <u>male characters</u>, but Belmont is <u>mainly associated</u> with <u>female characters</u>.

Music has an impact on the mood and atmosphere...

1) Music isn't used <u>a lot</u> in the play, but it helps to set the <u>atmosphere</u> of <u>certain scenes</u>.

2) In Belmont, <u>important</u> moments are often marked by music. For example, when the princes enter there is a "*Flourish of cornets*" — this makes their visits seem <u>significant</u> by creating a <u>ceremonial</u> atmosphere.

3) Music also plays while Bassanio takes the <u>casket test</u>. In this case, it makes the mood more <u>dramatic</u>.

4) In Act 5, Scene 1, "<u>sweet music</u>" is playing while Lorenzo tells Jessica about the <u>calming effect</u> music can have on a "<u>wild and wanton herd</u>" of animals. This creates a <u>serene</u> mood and helps to <u>ease the tension</u> from Act 4, Scene 1.

© United Archives GmbH / Alamy Stock Photo

> **Shakespeare's Techniques — Music**
>
> Music <u>isn't</u> used much in scenes set in <u>Venice</u>, but Shylock mentions it when he orders Jessica to <u>shut out</u> the sounds of the <u>masque</u> in Act 2, Scene 5. His desire to keep music out of his house contributes to its <u>oppressive atmosphere</u>.

... and so do references to time

1) By suggesting that time is <u>running out</u> for people, Shakespeare is able to create a <u>tense atmosphere</u>.

2) A <u>time limit</u> is placed on Antonio and Shylock's bond. Antonio is given <u>three months</u> to repay the loan and it's <u>two months</u> until his ships return, leaving <u>little margin</u> for anything to go <u>wrong</u>. This creates <u>suspense</u>.

3) Act 2, Scene 6 is <u>full</u> of references to time. Salerio says that Lorenzo's "<u>hour is almost past</u>" and Gratiano wants to be "under sail and gone <u>tonight</u>". This gives the scene an <u>urgent</u> atmosphere.

Think about how different moods are created...

The Merchant of Venice is a play of extremes — it can go from happy to sad or comic to tragic in the blink of an eye. You need to consider which techniques Shakespeare uses to bring about these changes in mood.

Dramatic Irony

It's a good thing that the audience knows what's going on — the characters often don't seem to have a clue...

Dramatic irony is created in different ways

1) Dramatic irony is where the audience knows something that one or more of the characters doesn't. In *The Merchant of Venice*, Shakespeare creates dramatic irony in different ways:

The audience hears private conversations containing information other characters don't know about yet.	Salerio and Solanio discuss rumours that one of Antonio's ships is wrecked (Act 2, Scene 8).
Characters reveal their thoughts in asides (see p.6).	Antonio thinks Shylock agrees to the loan out of kindness, but Shylock admits to the audience that he actually wants revenge (Act 1, Scene 3).
Characters wear disguises to hide who they really are — only the audience knows their true identity.	Bassanio and Gratiano fail to recognise their wives during the court scene (Act 4, Scene 1).

2) Dramatic irony makes the audience feel more involved, which helps to hold their attention.

3) It's closely linked to the recurring theme of appearance and reality (see p.40-41). Hidden motives and disguises reinforce the idea that appearances can be misleading.

It can cause tension...

1) Dramatic irony can be used to build suspense in the play.

2) It's used to create anticipation in Act 3, Scene 2 when Bassanio succeeds in the casket test. He's delighted, but the audience knows that his happiness will be short-lived — they hear about Antonio's losses in the previous scene.

3) Dramatic irony also builds tension in the court scene. The audience knows the true identity of the young lawyer and his assistant — they feel suspense as they wait to see if Portia saves Antonio without being found out.

© Donald Cooper/photostage

... but it can also create humour

1) Dramatic irony is the main source of humour towards the end of the play.

2) In Act 4, the audience enjoys seeing Bassanio and Gratiano fall into their wives' traps after they don't recognise Portia and Nerissa in their disguises.

Shakespeare's Techniques — Disguises

Plays are meant to be performed. The way the disguises look on stage is a big part of the humour they provide for the audience.

3) In Act 5, Scene 1, the audience knows that there's no need for Bassanio and Gratiano to get flustered by Portia and Nerissa's accusations. This makes their attempts to defend themselves entertaining.

KEY QUOTE *"What ring gave you my lord?"*

The audience doesn't need telling the answer to this question — they know that Portia's playing dumb to teach Bassanio a lesson. It works too, because Bassanio swears never to give his ring away... again.

Practice Questions

Congratulations for making it this far — your prize is a lovely set of practice questions. Admittedly it's not much of a prize, but your best bet is to work through them anyway. It's the only way of making sure it's all gone in...

Quick Questions

1) Give three common features of a comedy that are found in *The Merchant of Venice*.

2) How does swapping between different plots create suspense?

3) What is 'foreshadowing'?

4) What three rules does blank verse follow?

5) When you look at a passage, how can you tell if it's written in prose?

6) Why do the Christian characters sometimes call Shylock "the devil"?

7) Which casket has the inscription "Who chooseth me must give and hazard all he hath"?

8) Which technique is being used in this quote?
"There is more difference between thy flesh and hers than between jet and ivory".
a) repetition   b) personification   c) antithesis   d) simile

9) How are the princes' entrances given a ceremonial atmosphere?

10) Give one way that dramatic irony is created in the play.

In-depth Questions

1) Explain how *The Merchant of Venice* isn't a typical Shakespearean comedy.

2) Find an example of rhymed verse. Explain the effect rhyme has at this point in the play.

3) Choose a mythological image from the play and explain why you think it was used.

4) What is the significance of rings in the play?

5) Find a part of the play that has a tense atmosphere. How is this atmosphere created?

Practice Questions

You can't escape writing about techniques in the exam, so these questions are definitely worth doing. Look at them as a chance to show off what you've learnt in this section — you never know, you might impress yourself...

Exam-style Questions

1) Read the following extract. How does Shakespeare create humour in this extract and elsewhere in the play?

Lorenzo:	I shall grow jealous of you shortly, Lancelet, if you thus get my wife into corners.
Jessica:	Nay, you need not fear us, Lorenzo: Lancelet and I are out. He tells me flatly, there is no mercy for me in heaven, because I am a Jew's daughter: and he says, you are no good member of the commonwealth, for in converting Jews to Christians, you raise the price of pork.
Lorenzo:	I shall answer that better to the commonwealth than you can the getting up of the negro's belly: the Moor is with child by you, Lancelet.
Lancelet:	It is much that the Moor should be more than reason: but if she be less than an honest woman, she is indeed more than I took her for.
Lorenzo:	How every fool can play upon the word! I think the best grace of wit will shortly turn into silence, and discourse grow commendable in none only but parrots. Go in, sirrah; bid them prepare for dinner.
Lancelet:	That is done, sir; they have all stomachs.
Lorenzo:	Goodly Lord, what a wit-snapper are you? Then bid them prepare dinner.
Lancelet:	That is done too, sir; only 'cover' is the word.
Lorenzo:	Will you cover then, sir?
Lancelet:	Not so, sir, neither; I know my duty.

(Act 3, Scene 5)

2) Read Act 4, Scene 1 from "**Dear sir, of force I must attempt you further**" to "**away! Make haste**."

   a) What does this extract reveal about Bassanio's character?

   b) In this extract, Bassanio doesn't recognise Portia, which creates dramatic irony. Explain the importance of dramatic irony elsewhere in the play. You should consider:
   - when dramatic irony is used
   - the effect dramatic irony has on the play.

3) Read Act 3, Scene 3 from the start of the scene to "**Therefore he hates me.**"
   How does Shakespeare create a threatening mood in this extract and the rest of the play?

Exam Preparation

Getting to know the play will put you at a massive advantage in the exam. It's not enough just to read it though — you've got to get to grips with the nitty-gritty bits. It's all about gathering evidence...

The exam questions will test four main skills

You will need to show the examiner that you can:

1) Write about the text in a <u>thoughtful way</u> — <u>picking out</u> appropriate <u>examples</u> and <u>quotations</u> to back up your opinions.

2) <u>Identify</u> and <u>explain</u> features of the text's <u>form</u>, <u>structure</u> and <u>language</u>. Show how the author uses these to create <u>meanings</u> and <u>effects</u>.

3) Relate the text to its <u>cultural, social and historical background</u>.

4) Write in a <u>clear</u>, <u>well-structured</u> way. <u>5%</u> of the marks in your English Literature exams are for <u>spelling</u>, <u>punctuation</u> and <u>grammar</u>. Make sure that your writing is as <u>accurate</u> as possible.

Preparation is important

1) It's <u>important</u> to cover <u>all</u> the <u>different sections</u> of this book in your <u>revision</u>. You need to make sure you <u>understand</u> the text's <u>context</u>, <u>plot</u>, <u>characters</u>, <u>themes</u> and <u>writer's techniques</u>.

2) In the <u>exam</u>, you'll need to <u>bring together</u> your <u>ideas</u> about these topics to answer the question <u>quickly</u>.

3) Think about the different <u>characters</u> and <u>themes</u> in the text, and write down some <u>key points</u> and <u>ideas</u> about each one. Then, find some <u>evidence</u> to support each point — this could be something from <u>any</u> of the <u>sections</u> in this book. You could set out your evidence in a <u>table</u> like this:

Theme: Appearance and Reality	
Appearances can be misleading	The princes judge the value of the caskets according to what they look like, which is why they fail the test.
Characters	Characters aren't always as they seem — Portia is polite to her suitors in person, but judgmental of them in private.
Disguises	Disguises allow the characters to conceal their true identity — Portia and Nerissa both wear them in Act 4, Scene 1.
Language	Lots of imagery about deception, e.g. "Gilded tombs do worms enfold"
Form	The play isn't what an audience would expect from one of Shakespeare's comedies — the plot is much darker.

Preparing to succeed — a cunning plot indeed...

Knowing the plot inside out will be unbelievably helpful in the exam. It'll help you to stay calm and make sure you write a brilliant answer that positively glitters with little gems of evidence. The exam's just a chance for you to show off...

The Exam Question

This page deals with how to approach an exam question. The stuff below will help you get started on a scorching exam answer, more scorching than, say, a phoenix cooking fiery fajitas in a flaming furnace.

Read the question carefully and underline key words

1) The style of question you'll get depends on which <u>exam board</u> you're taking.

2) Read all the <u>instructions</u> carefully. Make sure you know <u>how many</u> questions you need to answer and <u>how much time</u> you should spend answering each one.

3) If the question has <u>more than one part</u>, look at the total number of marks for each bit. This should help you to plan your <u>time</u> in the exam.

4) <u>Read</u> the question at least <u>twice</u> so you completely understand it. <u>Underline</u> the key words. If you're given an <u>extract</u>, underline <u>important</u> words or phrases in that too.

Henry didn't read the weather report carefully enough when planning his weekend activities.

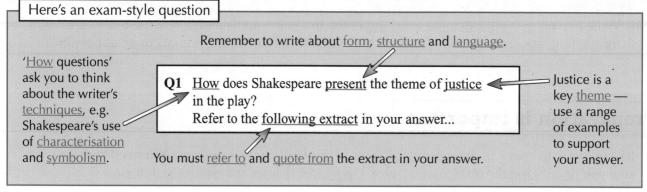

Here's an exam-style question

Remember to write about <u>form</u>, <u>structure</u> and <u>language</u>.

'<u>How</u> questions' ask you to think about the writer's <u>techniques</u>, e.g. Shakespeare's use of <u>characterisation</u> and <u>symbolism</u>.

Q1 <u>How</u> does Shakespeare <u>present</u> the theme of <u>justice</u> in the play?
Refer to the <u>following extract</u> in your answer...

Justice is a key <u>theme</u> — use a range of examples to support your answer.

You must <u>refer to</u> and <u>quote from</u> the extract in your answer.

When you're writing about an extract in the exam, some exam boards will ask you to focus only on that extract. Others will ask you to write about the extract and the text as a whole. Make sure you read the instructions carefully.

Get to know exam language

Some <u>words</u> come up time and again in <u>exam questions</u>. Have a look at some <u>specimen</u> papers, pick out words that are <u>often used</u> in questions and make sure that you <u>understand</u> what they mean. You could <u>write a few down</u> whilst you're revising. For example:

Question Word	You need to...
Explore / Explain	Show <u>how</u> the writer deals with a <u>theme</u>, <u>character</u> or <u>idea</u>. Make several <u>different</u> points to answer the question.
How does	Think about the <u>techniques</u> or <u>literary features</u> that the author uses to get their point across.
Give examples	Use <u>direct quotes</u> and describe <u>events</u> from the text in your own words.
Refer to	Read the question so that you know if you need to write about just an <u>extract</u>, or an extract and the <u>rest of the text</u>.

I've already got all the Marks I need — I know three...

Whatever question you're asked in the exam, your answer should touch on the main characters, themes, structure and language of the text. All the stuff we've covered in the rest of the book in fact. It's so neat, it's almost like we planned it.

Planning Your Answer

I'll say this once — and then I'll probably repeat it several times — it is absolutely, completely, totally and utterly essential that you make a plan before you start writing. Only a fool jumps right in without a plan...

Plan your answer before you start

Read through the extract carefully and annotate it with some ideas to help you make your plan.

1) If you plan, you're less likely to forget something <u>important</u>.

2) A good plan will help you <u>organise</u> your ideas — and write a good, <u>well-structured</u> essay.

3) Write your plan at the <u>top of your answer booklet</u> and draw a <u>neat line</u> through it when you've finished.

4) <u>Don't</u> spend <u>too long</u> on your plan. It's only <u>rough work</u>, so you don't need to write in full sentences. Here are a few <u>examples</u> of different ways you can plan your answer:

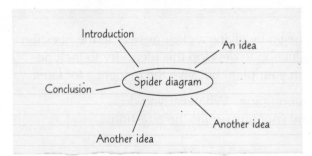

Bullet points...
- Introduction...
- An idea...
- The next idea...
- Another idea...
- Yet another idea...
- Conclusion...

Include bits of evidence in your plan

1) <u>Writing</u> your essay will be much <u>easier</u> if you include <u>important quotes</u> and <u>examples</u> in your plan.

2) You could include them in a <u>table</u> like this one:

A point...	Quote to back this up...
Another point...	Quote...
A different point...	Example...
A brand new point...	Quote...

3) <u>Don't</u> spend <u>too long</u> writing out quotes though. It's just to make sure you <u>don't forget</u> anything when you write your answer.

Structure your answer

Introduction
↓
Middle Section
— paragraphs
expanding
your
argument.
↓
Conclusion

1) Your <u>introduction</u> should give a brief answer to the question you're writing about. Make it clear how you're going to <u>tackle the topic</u>.

2) The <u>middle section</u> of your essay should explain your answer in detail and give evidence to back it up. Write a <u>paragraph</u> for each point you make. Make sure you <u>comment</u> on your evidence and <u>explain how</u> it helps to <u>prove</u> your point.

3) Remember to write a <u>conclusion</u> — a paragraph at the end which <u>sums up</u> your <u>main points</u>. There's <u>more</u> about introductions and conclusions on the <u>next page</u>.

Dirk finally felt ready to tackle the topic.

To plan or not to plan, that is the question...

The answer is yes, yes, a thousand times yes. Often students dive right in, worried that planning will take up valuable time. But 5 minutes spent organising a well-structured answer is loads better than pages of waffle. Mmm waffles.

Writing Introductions and Conclusions

Once you've written a plan like the one on p.59, you'll know what your main points are.
This will make writing your introduction and conclusion as easy as pie.

Get to the point straight away in your introduction

1) First, you need to <u>work out</u> what the question is <u>asking you</u> to do:

> ### How is the character of Antonio important to the play?
>
> The question is <u>asking you</u> to think about the <u>role</u> of <u>Antonio</u> in the play.
> Plan your essay by thinking about <u>how</u> this character <u>links</u> to the play's plot and main <u>themes</u>.

2) When you've <u>planned</u> your essay, you should <u>begin</u> by giving a <u>clear answer</u> to the <u>question</u> in a sentence or two. Use the <u>rest</u> of the <u>introduction</u> to <u>develop</u> this idea. Try to include the <u>main paragraph ideas</u> that you have listed in your plan, but <u>save</u> the <u>evidence</u> for later.

3) You could also use the <u>introduction</u> to give your <u>opinion</u>. Whatever you do, make sure your introduction makes it <u>clear</u> how your answer <u>fits the question</u>.

Your conclusion must answer the question

1) The <u>most important</u> thing you have to do at the <u>end</u> of your writing is to <u>summarise</u> your <u>answer</u> to the question.

2) It's your <u>last chance</u> to persuade the examiner, so make your <u>main point</u> again.

3) Use your <u>last sentence</u> to really <u>impress</u> the <u>examiner</u> — it will make your essay <u>stand out</u>. You could <u>develop</u> your own <u>opinion</u> of the text or <u>highlight</u> which of your <u>points</u> you thought was the most <u>interesting</u>.

The examiner was struggling to see the answer clearly.

Use the question words in your introduction and conclusion

1) Try to use <u>words</u> or <u>phrases</u> from the <u>question</u> in your introduction and conclusion.

> ### How does Shakespeare present wealth in the play?

2) This will show the examiner that you're <u>answering the question</u>.

> In 'The Merchant of Venice', Shakespeare presents wealth as the driving force behind many of the characters' actions. Money is often at the forefront of the characters' minds.

The first line of the introduction gives a clear answer, which will lead on to the rest of the essay.

3) This will also help you keep the question <u>fresh in your mind</u> so your answer doesn't <u>wander off-topic</u>.

I've come to the conclusion that I really like pie...

To conclude, the introduction eases the examiner in gently, whilst the conclusion is your last chance to impress.
But remember — the examiner doesn't want to see any new points lurking in those closing sentences.

Writing Main Paragraphs

So we've covered the beginning and the end, now it's time for the meaty bit. The roast beef in between the prawn cocktail and the treacle tart. This page is about how to structure your paragraphs. It's quite simple...

P.E.E.D. is how to put your argument together

Remember to start a new paragraph every time you make a new point.

1) P.E.E.D. stands for: Point, Example, Explain, Develop.

2) Begin each paragraph by making a point. Then give an example from the text (either a quote or a description). Next, explain how your example backs up your point.

3) Finally, try to develop your point by writing about its effect on the reader, how it links to another part of the text or what the writer's intention is in including it.

Use short quotes to support your ideas

1) Don't just use words from the play to show what happens in the plot...

> When Bassanio asks Antonio for money, Antonio tells him "My purse, my person, my extremest means, / Lie all unlocked to your occasions".

This just gives an example from the text without offering any explanation or analysis.

2) Instead, it's much better to use short quotes as evidence to support a point you're making.

3) It makes the essay structure clearer and smoother if most quotes are embedded in your sentences.

It's better to use short, embedded quotes as evidence. Then you can go on to explain them.

> Antonio values friendship over money. He offers his "purse" and "extremest means" to help Bassanio woo Portia. He doesn't question how much money Bassanio needs or why he needs it, but says his wealth is "unlocked" to him.

Get to know some literary language

1) Using literary terms in your answer will make your essay stand out — as long as you use them correctly.

2) When you're revising, think about literary terms that are relevant to the text and how you might include them in an essay. Take a look at the table below for some examples.

Literary Term	Definition	Example
Personification	A figure of speech that talks about a thing as if it's a person.	"How sweet the moonlight sleeps upon this bank!"
Simile	Compares one thing to another, often using 'like' and 'as'.	"her sunny locks / Hang on her temples like a golden fleece"
Metaphor	Describes something by saying it is something else.	"Our house is hell"

This page is so exciting — I nearly...

Now now, let's all be grown-ups and avoid the obvious joke. It's a good way of remembering how to structure your paragraphs though. Point, Example, Explain, Develop. Simple. Maybe we could make a rap or something... anyone?

In the Exam

Keeping cool in the exam can be tricky. But if you take in all the stuff on this page, you'll soon have it down to a fine art. Then you can stroll out of that exam hall with the swagger of an essay-writing master.

Don't panic if you make a mistake

1) Okay, so say you've timed the exam beautifully. Instead of putting your feet up on the desk for the last 5 minutes, it's a good idea to <u>read through</u> your <u>answers</u> and <u>correct any mistakes</u>...

2) If you want to get rid of a mistake, <u>cross it out</u>. <u>Don't scribble</u> it out as this can look messy. Make any corrections <u>neatly</u> and <u>clearly</u> instead of writing on top of the words you've already written.

> techniques
> The author uses various literary ~~teknikues~~ to explore this theme.

This is the clearest way to correct a mistake. Don't be tempted to try writing on top of the original word.

3) If you've <u>left out</u> a <u>word</u> or a <u>phrase</u> and you've got space to add it in, write the missing bit <u>above</u> the line with a '^' to show <u>exactly</u> where it should go.

Re-read the sentence carefully to work out where the '^' symbol needs to go.

> and hyperbole
> The writer uses imagery to draw attention to this point.

4) If you've left out whole <u>sentences</u> or <u>paragraphs</u>, write them in a <u>separate section</u> at the <u>end</u> of the essay. Put a <u>star</u> (*) next to both the <u>extra writing</u> and the <u>place</u> you want it to go.

Always keep an eye on the time

1) It's surprisingly <u>easy</u> to <u>run out of time</u> in exams. You've got to leave <u>enough time</u> to answer <u>all</u> the questions you're asked to do. You've also got to leave enough time to <u>finish</u> each essay properly — with a <u>clear ending</u>.

2) Here are some <u>tips</u> on how to <u>avoid</u> running out of time:

- Work out <u>how much time</u> you have for each part of your answer <u>before</u> you <u>start</u>.
- Take off a few minutes at the beginning to <u>plan</u>, and a <u>few minutes</u> at the end for your <u>conclusion</u>.
- Make sure you have a <u>watch</u> to <u>time yourself</u> — and keep checking it.
- Be <u>strict</u> with yourself — if you spend <u>too long</u> on one part of your answer, you may run out of time.
- If you're <u>running out of time</u>, keep <u>calm</u>, <u>finish</u> the <u>point</u> you're on and move on to your <u>conclusion</u>.

Stephanie never had a problem with keeping cool.

Treat an exam like a spa day — just relax...

Some people actually do lose the plot when they get into the exam. The trick is to keep calm and well... carry on. If you make sure you get your exam technique sorted, you'll be as relaxed as a sloth in a room full of easy chairs.

Sample Exam Question

And now the bit you've all been waiting for — a sample exam question and a lovely little plan.
Go and make yourself a cup of tea, then settle down and enjoy.

Here's a sample exam question...

Read this feisty exam question. That's the best way to start...

In the exam, you'll be given the full extract in the exam paper.

Read the question carefully. Underline the important bits.

The focus here is on how Portia is presented — you'll need to think about the language she uses, how she behaves and what the other characters say about her.

Q1 Read Act 4, Scene 1 from "**Do you confess the bond**?" to "**The penalty and the forfeit of my bond**." How does Shakespeare present Portia in this extract and elsewhere in the play?

You'll need to discuss the passage given in detail, but you also need to refer to the rest of the play.

Back up each point with evidence from the text and analyse the effect it has on your impression of Portia.

Here's how you could plan your answer

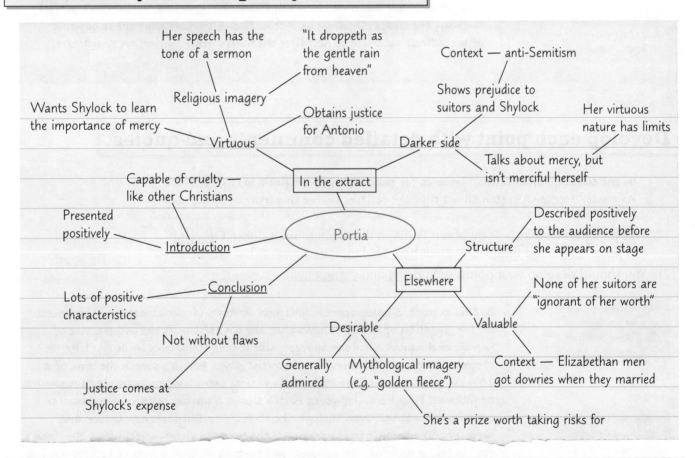

What do examiners eat? Why, egg-sam-wiches of course...

The most important thing to remember is DON'T PANIC. Take a deep breath, read the question, read it again, write a plan... take another deep breath... and start writing. Leave a few minutes at the end to check your answer too.

Section Six — Exam Advice

Worked Answer

These pages will show you how to take an OK answer and turn it into a great one that will really impress the examiner.

Use your introduction to get off to a good start

These pages are all about how to word your sentences to impress the examiner, so we haven't included everything from the plan on p.63.

You might start with something like:

> In 'The Merchant of Venice', Shakespeare presents Portia as a virtuous character. Her role in saving Antonio's life makes her the source of a lot of happiness in the play. Portia is also rich and beautiful, which explains why she is sought-after by so many suitors.

1) This introduction is <u>okay</u>. It looks at the <u>character</u> of Portia and how she is <u>presented</u>.

2) Using the <u>key words</u> from the question gives your essay <u>focus</u>, and shows the examiner that you're on <u>track</u> and thinking about the question from the start.

3) However, there's still room for <u>improvement</u> — here's a better introduction:

This tells the examiner that you've thought about Portia's role in the play.

> As the heroine of 'The Merchant of Venice', Portia is generally presented positively. Her decisive actions help to avoid a tragic ending, which makes her a source of happiness in the play. In the extract, Portia is shown to be a virtuous character. She powerfully defends the importance of mercy in a selfless attempt to save Antonio's life. Elsewhere in the play, she is presented as desirable. Her wealth and beauty mean that she is sought-after by Bassanio and other suitors. However, Portia isn't perfect. The way she treats Shylock in Act 4, Scene 1 shows that she is capable of prejudice and cruelty, just like the play's other Christian characters.

This shows a detailed understanding of Portia's character.

Develop each point with detailed comments and quotes

> In the extract, Portia seems virtuous for encouraging Shylock to take pity on Antonio. Her long speech shows that she believes in the importance of mercy.

1) This paragraph makes a <u>point</u> about Portia in the extract, but it doesn't <u>develop</u> this point <u>fully</u> or go into detail about <u>how</u> Shakespeare presents her character.

2) You should develop your points with <u>detail</u> and <u>comments</u>:

This makes a relevant point about the extract, and then goes on to provide evidence.

> In this extract, Shakespeare highlights Portia's virtuous nature. Her speech on the "quality of mercy" shows that she understands the importance of mercy and wants Shylock to recognise it too. Religious imagery like "It droppeth as the gentle rain from heaven" gives Portia's speech the tone of a sermon, which makes her attitude to mercy seem like an example that should be followed by others. However, Portia shows a darker side to her character later in this scene. Even though she stresses to Shylock how important mercy is, she doesn't try to persuade the Duke to show mercy when Shylock's fate is being decided. This shows that Portia's virtuous nature has its limits.

This shows a good knowledge of where the extract comes from in the play.

Referring back to the question keeps your answer focused.

Worked Answer

Write about the rest of the play

In this question, you can't just focus on the extract — you need to discuss Portia elsewhere in the play.

> Elsewhere in the play, the way other characters talk about Portia makes her seem sought-after. Bassanio's speech in Act 1, Scene 1 suggests that her wealth is what makes her so desirable.

1) This paragraph still focuses on how Portia is presented but discusses the rest of the play.
2) You can make this paragraph better by giving more detailed examples and backing up points with quotes.

> Elsewhere in the play, the way other characters talk about Portia makes her seem desirable. In Act 1, Scene 1, Bassanio uses mythological imagery to describe her to Antonio. He compares Portia to the "golden fleece" and her suitors to "Jasons", which presents her as a rare prize worth taking risks for. The fact that there are several "Jasons" competing for her hand in marriage suggests that she isn't just greatly valued by Bassanio, but is also generally admired. Furthermore, Bassanio describes Portia using language related to money. He tells Antonio that none of her suitors are "ignorant of her worth". This emphasises that her wealth is an important part of her appeal.

Remember to show that you know the play as a whole.

This develops the point about what Bassanio's language tells us about Portia.

3) You could develop this by focusing on the context in which the play was written:

> In the 16th century, a bride's family often gave a dowry (a sum of money or property) to the man marrying her. Bassanio describes Portia as "richly left", so her dowry is likely to be large. This makes her even more desirable as a wife.

Make sure any points about context are linked closely to both the text and the question.

Finish your essay in style

You could say:

> In 'The Merchant of Venice', Portia is a virtuous and desirable character who is largely responsible for the play's happy ending. However, she's also prejudiced and capable of cruelty.

1) This conclusion is okay, but it doesn't summarise how Shakespeare presents Portia.
2) To make it really impressive, you could say something like:

> In 'The Merchant of Venice', Portia's virtuous nature presents her as a moral example for other characters to follow. In the extract, her powerful speech shows that she genuinely wants Shylock to recognise the importance of mercy. The audience sees more of Portia's positive characteristics elsewhere in the play. Other characters praise her and desire her, and she's ultimately responsible for the happy ending to the play. However, Portia isn't without flaws. She may deliver justice for Antonio, but she does it at Shylock's expense.

This shows that you've considered several aspects of Portia's character.

Make your final sentence really stand out — it's your last opportunity to impress the examiner.

Why do alligators write good essays? Their quotes are so snappy...

It seems like there's a lot to remember on these two pages, but there's not really. To summarise — write a scorching intro and a sizzling conclusion, make a good range of points (one per paragraph) and include plenty of examples. Easy.

Index

A

anti-Semitism 43, 46
antithesis 39, 52
Antonio 9, 11, 15, 16, 18, 20-22, 25, 36, 37, 39, 40, 42, 43, 46, 51
appearances 14, 15, 17, 22, 29, 33, 40, 41
atmosphere 10, 22, 29, 30, 48, 49, 53

B

Bassanio 9-12, 17, 20-22, 26, 38, 39, 41, 42, 48-51
Belmont 10, 53
Bible 36
blank verse 12, 48, 49

C

caskets 10, 14, 15, 17, 22, 26, 33, 39, 41, 42, 47, 48, 51
Christianity 11, 13, 16, 19-21, 25, 28, 29, 33, 36-38, 43, 50, 51
comedies 6, 12, 22, 46
commercial imagery 50
conclusions 60, 65
conflict 1, 11, 17, 26, 29, 39, 43, 50
courtly love 38

D

daughters 13, 15, 27, 29, 38, 39, 42
disguises 13, 19, 20, 22, 41, 46, 54
dramatic irony 11, 21, 22, 41, 54
Duke 18, 20, 21, 33, 40, 42

E

exam advice 57-65

F

fathers 10, 12, 13, 16, 27, 29, 38, 39, 46, 51
foreshadowing 20, 47
form 46
friendship 9, 17, 25, 26, 30, 39, 51

G

Globe Theatre 2
Gratiano 12, 14, 22, 31, 37, 38, 41, 46, 51

H

humour 10, 12, 19, 21, 22, 32, 47, 52, 54
hyperbole 12, 25, 52

I

iambic pentameter 48, 49
imagery 12, 20, 22, 29, 31, 33, 43, 49-51
introductions 60, 64

J

Jessica 13, 14, 16, 19, 22, 28, 29, 38-40, 42, 47, 49
Judaism 11, 13, 16, 19, 25, 28, 29, 31, 36-38, 42, 43, 50
justice 17, 20, 21, 28, 33, 36, 37, 50, 51

L

Lancelet 12, 19, 32, 48, 52
laws 18, 20, 33, 36, 40, 51
loans 11, 42
Lorenzo 13, 14, 19, 22, 29, 31, 38, 49
love 1, 15, 17, 22, 26, 31, 38, 39, 46, 47, 50
loyalty 17, 21, 26, 31, 32, 41, 51

M

malapropisms 32
marriage 26, 27, 29, 38, 42, 46, 50
mercy 1, 17, 20, 21, 33, 36, 37, 40
metaphors 14, 50, 61
mockery 10, 15, 16, 19, 37, 43
money 9, 11, 12, 15, 16, 18, 20, 25, 26, 29, 31, 38, 39, 42
moneylending 11
mood 9, 10, 13, 15-17, 20, 22, 47, 53
music 22, 33, 53
mythological imagery 12, 22, 50

N

Nerissa 21, 22, 30, 38, 39, 41, 49

P

personification 13, 50, 61
planning 59, 63
poems 14, 15, 38, 41, 48
Portia 10, 12, 14, 17-22, 27, 37-41, 43, 49, 50, 52, 63-65
pound of flesh 11, 21, 28, 37, 51
prejudice 25, 27, 28, 31-33, 43, 46
Prince of Aragon 15, 33, 41, 51
Prince of Morocco 12, 14, 33, 40, 41
prose 7, 10, 12, 32, 48, 49
punishments 21, 28, 33, 37, 40
puns 19, 52

R

religious imagery 20, 50
repetition 9, 27, 52
revenge 1, 16, 18, 20, 25, 28, 36, 37, 43, 51
rhymed verse 48
rhythm 7, 48, 49
rings 16, 17, 21, 22, 26, 30, 39, 41, 47, 51
romance 22, 29, 31, 38, 39, 42, 48
rumours 15, 16, 54

S

sadness 9, 10, 13, 25, 27, 31, 32, 39
Salerio 15, 16, 32
settings 10, 20, 42, 53
Shakespeare 1
Shylock 11-13, 15-18, 20, 21, 25, 28, 36, 37, 39, 40, 42, 43, 46, 49-51
similes 50, 61
Solanio 15, 16, 32
stage directions 6
structure 11, 12, 17, 46, 47
sub-plots 42, 46, 47
suspense 10, 12, 15, 19, 47, 53, 54
symbolism 51

T

tension 10, 11, 14, 15, 17-19, 32, 36, 47, 49, 50, 52-54
time 10, 14, 18, 43, 53
tragedies 6, 46
tricks 12, 21, 22, 27, 30, 39, 47, 54
Tubal 16, 39

U

usury 42

V

Venice 2, 18, 28, 33, 36, 38, 41-43, 53
victims 11, 15, 16, 25, 28, 29, 46
villains 11, 16, 21, 28, 46, 50

W

wealth 9, 16, 27, 38, 42
women 20, 27, 38, 41, 53
worked answer 64, 65

Index

The Characters in 'The Merchant of Venice'

Phew! You should be an expert on *The Merchant of Venice* by now. But if you want a bit of light relief and a quick recap of what happens in the play, read through *The Merchant of Venice — The Cartoon...*

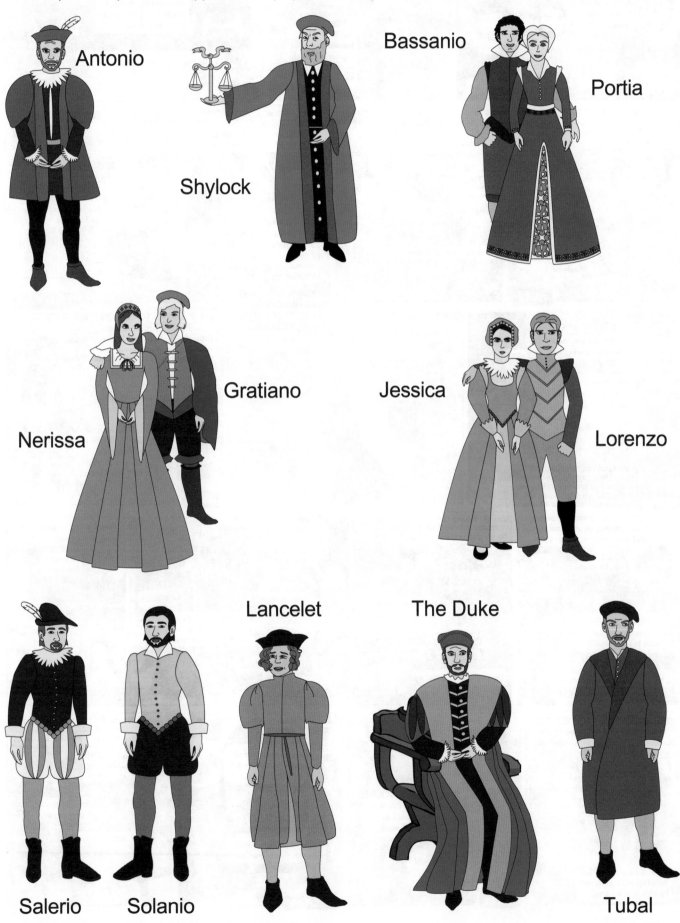

Antonio

Shylock

Bassanio

Portia

Nerissa

Gratiano

Jessica

Lorenzo

Lancelet

The Duke

Salerio

Solanio

Tubal

William Shakespeare's 'The Merchant of Venice'

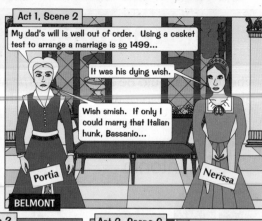

ETMV41